Foreword by Rev. Joe Kim

Boundless
LOVE

Healing Your Marriage Before It Begins

CHRISTINA & JAVIER LLERENA

Interior design: Matias Baldanza.

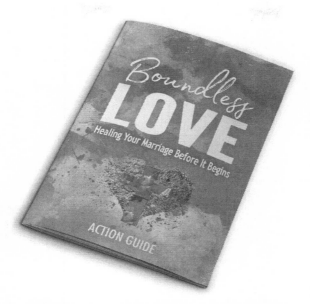

FREE ACTION GUIDE!

Read This First

We've found that readers get the most success with this book when they use the Action Guide as they read along and after finishing the book.

And, just to say thanks for downloading our book, we'd love to give you the Action Guide for FREE!

TO DOWNLOAD, GO TO:
www.boundlesslove.us/actionguide

DEDICATION

Javier

TO OUR HEAVENLY FATHER. You never left me.

To my daughters, Isabel ("Pledged to God") and Lucia ("Graceful Light.") You are my greatest accomplishment in my life. Thank you for giving me the gift of being your father on Earth.

To Sheila and Luis, for friendship, brotherhood, and sisterhood. I am deeply grateful for our relationship. Thank you for introducing Christina to me. I love you! I am so grateful for being part of your life. I am forever in your debt for making mine so boundless.

To my siblings Maria, Eduardo, Alicia, and Miguel—we fought a good fight!

Christina

TO OUR DAUGHTERS, Isabel Paulina and Lucia Maria, may you always remember that you are precious in the eyes of God and you are fully loved no matter what you do. You are daughters of the one true King and always protected. We love you with all our hearts and are so thankful that you chose us to be your parents.

To my parents, Paul and Loretta, who gave me everything and more. Thank you for always supporting my dreams and being my biggest fans. Your commitment to one another serves as a living example of unconditional love in action.

To our Heavenly Father. Thank you for holding us in the palm of your hand and loving us as your precious children. We give you all the glory and all the gratitude in our hearts. May our words glorify you and all your gifts.

CONTENTS

CONTENTS

CONTENTS

FOREWORD I

IF WE WERE TO NAME the top reasons why people today fear commitment, they might include: I'll get hurt just like before and it's hard to trust, it won't work out anyway because I've seen too many failures including myself, I wouldn't be free anymore and it's not my definition of fun, I'm too young and that's for old people, it's way too big of a decision, I'm good with my life now, and why add complications. All these are legitimate, and I have heard them or felt them myself. In my work as a priest, I have assisted all sorts of people in making major decisions (what to do, what not to do, how, when, why). I've noticed that for those who have made a decision that they are happy with (including myself), the most helpful thing was seeking the advice of people who have made the decision already.

This is what the Prophet Jeremiah says, "Stand by the roads, and look, and ask for the ancient paths, where the good way is; and walk in it, and find rest for your souls" (6:16). Not that the advice of people will make our decision for us, but that we might begin to imagine and see ourselves more clearly in an otherwise dark, confusing future. Not that these people were perfect, either. Rather they felt the same things, got hurt in the same way, made some mistakes along the way, and made realizations about themselves, about life, and about the concept of perfection. Javier and Christina are those people. Their story is not about two perfect people, rather how God brought two people to perfection through marriage.

The biblical understanding of perfection is beatitude or fulfillment—becoming what we were originally created to be. Unfortunately, there are a whole lot of bad things in the world (and in us) that derail us from perfection. However, marriage is one of the ancient gifts of God that was never taken away or completely destroyed by any evil (thank God). In fact, you could read the entire history of humanity as God's plan to restore marriage to its original glory—a completely transparent, loving interchange of love between persons which creates something new. The suffering, death, and resurrection of Jesus Christ is the action of the love of a spouse in the face of some horrible infidelity. That kind of love is trustworthy, stable, freeing, dependable, refreshing, renewing, and best of all, without end. Where is this love and is it even possible today? You'll find a description in the following pages. You'll find it waiting within you.

—Rev. Joseph Kim,
Diocese of San Jose, California.

"God became one of us, so we could become like unto God."
—Feast of St Athanasius

FOREWORD II

THE BIBLICAL CONCEPT OF A man and a woman being bonded together shows its roots in Genesis 2:18, "The Lord God said, "It is not good for the man to be alone. I will make a helper suitable for him." God decides that man cannot do it alone and needs a "helper." (Don't get caught up on the word "helper"—it was not intended as a negative term and is also used by God to describe Himself.) God recognizes that navigating through life can be tough, complicated, and sometimes lonely—life can be easier when two people are working together toward a common goal. Later in Genesis 2:24-25, the author explains the point of marriage: two people leave their past lives behind and are joined together to go through life as if they are one. Put yourself in the "shoes" of Adam and Eve at this point in their marriage. At the point of how God originally desired marriage to look. In verse 25, the man and the woman are completely exposed, vulnerable, and intimate with each other without shame. Emotionally, spiritually, physically, they had nothing to hide from themselves, each other, or from God. Now imagine what your marriage could look like if that image was the goal.

Adam and Eve went on to face life together including its ups, downs, temptations, challenges, and joys—your marriage will as well. "Marriage isn't easy" is advice given to every young couple by just about everyone who has been married. You are probably sick of hearing it. However, it is such a common piece of advice for a reason: because it is absolutely true. When you get married your spouse will begin to know things about you that you are not even aware of yourself. The knowledge, however, is not what makes marriage tough, it is your willingness to be exposed, vulnerable and intimate with yourself, with your spouse, and with God that makes it so hard. It takes effort, practice, and often, the example of others. In the time that I have known them, I have experienced Christina and Javier to be one of those couples who have the gift of openness, honesty, and of vulnerability about themselves, their marriage, and their faith. As you read this book, I encourage you to not only collect information about marriage and how to prepare; I encourage you to look to how Christina and Javier share about themselves as well. Learn from them and their experience. Christina and Javier have been through the ups and downs, temptations, challenges, and joys. One of my favorite things about this book is that it is not just a plan for a good marriage, nor is it simply a collection of good advice—it is Christina and Javier being emotionally exposed, vulnerable, and intimate with you. This is a rare opportunity for you to hear from a couple who have spent time reflecting, praying, and working on themselves and their relationship. I pray that you engage and learn as much from them and this book as I have.

—Mark Juanes,
Global Servant. Sunnyvale, California.

INTRODUCTION

"Be completely humble and gentle; be patient, bearing with one another in love."

—Ephesians 4:2 (ESV)

Marriage Gets No Love

You probably know that marriage gets minimal props these days. Sure, on the one hand, we still romanticize it as a symbol of love, while on the other hand, criticizing it for its lackluster success rate. It's a sad story that is reproduced in the media with the cryptic message: "Good luck—you've got a 50/50 shot at best. Have at it!"

Divorce rates in the United States hover between 40 and 50 percent depending on which state you live, the age that you marry, and your level of education. Hey, we get it. Relationships are messy, complicated, extremely personal, and can kick your butt whether you're married or not.

However, this depiction is not one that empowers you or your partner to feel pumped, let alone confident about getting married. We aim to change that. Marriage can be the best thing that ever happens to you and through you.

Don't Believe the Hype

Marriage is fulfilling, fun, expectation-busting, mind-blowing, and if you include God, spiritually transformative. Believing in the best possible outcome in marriage is actually countercultural because you are not following the pack. Instead, you are forging your own path together—a path that can be bigger than you ever imagined. If you put faith first—at the core of your relationship commitment—you put your marriage on a whole other level.

Building your marriage upon your faith is the secret to success—anything is possible with God. By not letting your flawed and imperfect humanity call the shots in your marriage, you are ahead of the game. So good on you for even picking this book up!

"A great marriage begins by becoming a greater follower of Jesus Christ."

—BETH STEFFANIAK

This book is for those who are single, dating, not dating, and engaged—basically anyone who is not married *yet*! In their heart of hearts, they desire to be married and are open to a spiritually-based marriage. This may be due to a well-established relationship with God or a spiritual community. This may also be due to spiritual curiosity. And for many, it is due to a spiritual thirst for deeper meaning in their primary adult relationship—one that will last throughout their lives.

Bottom line: this book is for anyone at any part of the spiritual dating/relationship journey!

It doesn't matter if you are single, dating, or not even engaged right now. All that matters is that you are open to including your relationship with God into your current or future relationship with your life partner. Our testimony is that your marriage will not only survive but thrive, grow, and flourish. You will be a very different person in the process. Who's not down for that?!

To have an awesome, outta-the-park, joyful marriage, you can't fall for the statistical predictions or even sub-par, real-life examples of marriage around you now. Divorce rates hover around 45 percent, polls show that young adults under thirty have less confidence in tying the knot than their grandmothers did, and the success rate declines the more times you marry. On top of that, millennials are leading the way by foregoing marriage altogether and simply cohabitating. More and more, we're being taught that marriage won't deliver the happiness we want.

If you are blessed to have amazing marriages to model, that's awesome but not always the norm. Put on the armor of God and roll with a new mindset and let's jump-start your marriage for greatness!

Instead of a "may the odds be ever in your favor" mindset, hold onto the truth that God wants success, joy, and peace in your marriage. This book is our invitation to bring your faith into your marriage before you actually get married. We want to prepare your heart, mind, and soul for a relationship that heals, blesses, and inspires you with awesome personal growth and an amazing life together.

Our spiritual mission is to help prepare you for a marriage that few have or talk about—one of deep connection, friendship, intimacy, and boundless love. Being vulnerable is scary and no easy task. We get it. We live it. We fail. Every. Day. But our failures make us smarter, stronger, and—far from breaking us—begin to build us up.

Don't sweat it! God has got this. There are no coincidences, only Divine order. The transformational power inherent in a spiritually-based marriage far outweighs the daily struggles and life's rough patches ahead.

Boundless love means to experience a love beyond what you originally thought possible in marriage. In Matthew, Jesus says that church members should forgive each other "seventy times seven times" (18:22), a number that symbolizes boundlessness.

Unconditional love tests the limits of our consciousness and our ability to forgive. Boundless love exceeds your current situation or what you've witnessed as possible in a relationship. It's that age-old realization, "I don't know what I don't know." What God has in store for our marriages is far better than what we can create or imagine.

Boundless love is about healing oneself and seeing marriage as a vehicle for change in every area of your life. No one says marriage is easy. We get that. But boundless love is about what you really, really want in your marriage.

INTRODUCTION

What you really want in your marriage is rooted in what you truly value. Do you aspire to have the kind of marriage that brings you closer to God, builds you up, and encourages you (sometimes in a tough love kind of way) to be a better person? Do you want a relationship that is a fortress of safety, peace, and encouragement?

Not many people talk about the lifelong opportunities experienced in marriage. We more often get a risk assessment complete with potential collateral damage. We get no guidebook or example of how it can actually function or go right. We know; marriage is not for the weak. It can feel like an emotional marathon. Yet, boundless love awaits at every rest stop.

> *"Before you marry someone, you should first make them use a computer with slow internet to see who they are."*
>
> —Anonymous

We attract our partner into our lives to heal us. God uses him/her to perfectly bring out our spiritual greatness. A lot of sludge comes to the surface along the way. Your "person" is perfect for you, even when it doesn't quite feel that way.

Not everyone may applaud your relationship. In fact, many relationships are tested early on by family, friends, and faith in each other. Having God as your foundation in your partnership will not only propel you forward in the right direction but also provide a richer context for why conflict happens and what gifts lay behind it.

Rewards, gifts, and blessings can be so much greater than all the failing statistics and bad examples abundant in our daily lives. We believe in you and we believe in God. True statement. Nothing is impossible. And we pray that you will feel empowered, uplifted, and ready to rock your marriage with your honey and faith at your side.

Our book reads with two narrators. We share our unique perspectives in each chapter based on our individual life lenses. Each section will be marked, so please know that we are sharing two unique versions of the reality that leads to our marriage.

After reading *Boundless Love*, our prayer, wish, and goal for you is to:

1) Love and accept yourself fully as God does;
2) Forgive and heal your childhood;
3) Know when to say yes or no and stick by your boundaries;
4) Cultivate, embrace, and act on your values and what matters most;
5) Honor the process of courtship and the gift of mutual respect;
6) Experience sexual intimacy beyond sex;
7) Talk openly and honestly about money in your relationship;
8) Forgive yourself and others for past hurts.
9) Envision your marriage and faith flourishing together!

Here begins a new relationship, a new promise, and an exciting, blessed marriage for a lifetime and eternity.

So let's be boundless. Dig in, get a cup of coffee or tea on your own or with your sweetie, and let's go!

XOXO, Christina & Javier

CHAPTER 1

Loving Me, Myself, and I

*"Whoever gets sense loves his own soul; he
who keeps understanding will discover good."*

—Proverbs 19:8 (ESV)

Loving Yourself Is Not Selfish

(CHRISTINA)

One message that I received growing up was, "You are so selfish!" As a strong-headed, feisty Midwestern teenager in the '80s, I wasn't exactly aware of how my behavior came across to my parents and sister. I knew that being "selfish" was not a compliment and definitely not something you want to be called by the people you love.

Many of us have "luggage" (as Javier likes to say) when it comes to the concept and practice of self-love. "Self-love" may feel awkward, self-helpish, hippy-dippy. . . you get the picture.

11

I thought that loving myself was being selfish and not okay. "Who am I to love me? All I see are my mistakes, shortcomings, and faults. I have to work harder to prove myself so I can find a partner who will love me. I need to *fix* myself so I *deserve* love."

I was driven. Determined to be worthy to receive romantic love, my overachieving personality-on-steroids kicked in. Work out, get a good job, join a dating site. I told myself that if I could just do enough and achieve enough, then I would earn love and be rewarded with a life partner.

It took some time, but gradually I learned that, thankfully, this is not how God works. And it is not how self-love works. You cannot control, earn, or force your way to an amazing relationship and marriage. God is in control (not you) and surrendering this sooner makes the path a lot less painful.

Of course, it is healthy to look at your past relationships and childhood and reflect on your values and what you truly want in a partner. However, we cross a line when we start to feel that we need to work our way to worthiness or bargain with God in order to attract a partner when, deep down, we don't recognize our innate worthiness in God's eyes.

I learned this after spending many years away from God. When I was twenty-eight years old, I decided to get back on the Christianity bus. I spent a lot of time wandering and searching, and then I found a church to call home. My burdens lightened and my heart softened. God and I got reacquainted.

Soon, I discovered that His love covers all the bases. I am precious in His eyes and am automatically worthy just by being alive. It was a big momma, lightbulb, Thank You Jesus moment.

You Are Lovable by Birthright

(CHRISTINA)

I am worthy because I'm a child of God—warts, calluses, stretch marks, mistakes, wrong turns, and all. Done deal. Stop stressing. That internalization pretty much changed my life forever and always.

I began to really dig into my prospects. Instead of going on Match.com and dating strangers, I decided to date myself. Yep, self and I needed to get right. I "took a break from dating." All my previous relationships ended in disaster so why not try something new?

The con was over. I knew that my primary relationship was between God and me. I didn't have to earn it. I eased into this idea—it's all good and it's all God—and it doesn't matter who you are or what you thought or what you did before.

Self-love is the magic formula for a deeply-connected and intimate relationship or marriage. I'm sure you've heard, "You can't give what you don't have." It is the foundation, the big enchilada, the first master lesson of finding your true partner in life.

> *"You yourself, as much as anybody in the entire universe, deserve your love and affection."*
>
> —Buddha

Faith was a huge part of this for me. Meditation, prayer, affirmations, and therapy were game-changers in moving me into higher consciousness. And, I prayed and prayed and prayed.

Not to find "Mr. Right" but to become "Ms. Right" and that was a whole different banana.

If you want love, give it graciously to yourself. Be generous, not stingy, and feed your primary relationships—with God and your new BFF, you. By holding yourself up to a new standard of conditional love, you open the door for blessings to come into your life.

The truth was shocking to me. I gave love and forgiveness to everyone else first, and I maybe got the leftovers. You have to nurture yourself to be a vessel and messenger of God. There is no other way. At the end of the day, who can be with you if you cannot fully be with yourself?

We invite you to take your self-love temperature. Is it cold and clammy or hot and on the rise? Who do you see when you look in the mirror? Wink at yourself in the mirror and say, "Hello, sexy beast!" after you wake up. You will crack a smile.

Do you enjoy your own company? I learned to love to go out to dinner and enjoy a movie by myself. I truly appreciated my own companionship with God at my side. The silence, the stillness, and the pure simplicity of hanging out alone became a joy.

God doesn't have to be found in someone else first. He is in you and with you, all the time. My ability to love me changed my world. It reframed my view of others and they began to treat me differently.

Our prayer for you is that you love yourself as God adores you—wholly, fully, and unconditionally. Yes, it is a lifetime of work, but start with giving yourself some mercy. With Him at your side, your marriage will move your self-love dial so that when you lose sight of your perfection—because you will—you will reconcile this illusion more quickly and frequently.

What Is the Story You Tell Yourself?

(JAVIER)

As a child, I remember when the summer started, my Dad arranged a month-long vacation. One time during the six-hour drive, I decided to count every tree I saw from the time I left my home to the house that we rented by the beach. That summer was memorable. I wrote down the number of trees and how many times my dad made me laugh.

Now that I look back, I see how important it is to capture the good in life and write it down. We are often absorbed by digital technology, emails, notifications, alerts, and the daily grind. We can overlook the good inside of us and in our lives.

I started journaling daily nine years ago. I wrote in a notebook every morning about what was happening in my life—my struggles and victories. I covered it all from the birth of my first daughter to the time when my startup CEO boss fled the country and left me and my fellow employees without a paycheck.

I eventually realized that I typed the same storylines over and over in my entries like "I've gotten fat and it's hard to lose weight at my age!" I focused on continual complaints like, "Why can't I get the job of my dreams?" My journal was a depressing song on repeat.

Every entry had the same theme: struggle. The same old problems didn't go away. Once in a while, a bit of personal praise or mention of victories popped in, but it was too rare to be uplifting.

It became clear that I felt no self-love at all. Perhaps because of that, it was easy to blame the world for my insecurities, health challenges, career struggles, and relationship conflicts.

I was my own judge and jury, sentencing myself again and again to misery. Compassion was missing in my life—compassion for myself. I was a loving husband and father, but what about me? I wasn't encouraging myself or looking for the wins from day to day. I wasn't grateful or thanking God for the gift of life every day.

Loving Yourself Makes Miracles Happen

(JAVIER)

I tend to think of myself as an extrovert. I love talking to people and sharing my stories, and yes, giving all the suggestions I can. I also suffer from social anxiety. Every time I am in a social setting where I don't know people, I go into my head.

Questions come up. Do they like me? Are they okay with what I am sharing? Do I fit in? The more I doubt myself, the more I see people becoming distanced. The more I accept myself for who I am, the more interactions become natural. It is truly incredible that how we feel about ourselves can change our surroundings.

Miracles happen when you start loving yourself. When you shut down the voices in your head that are constantly judging and protecting you from the truth of who you really are, you open yourself to the moment. You see more clearly.

It sounds weird, doesn't it? I can say out loud, "Javier, I love you." Or give myself a high five. "I am amazing!" But it's more than a moment of praise. It is about cultivating patience and gentleness with yourself, knowing that you are a worthwhile human being who deserves forgiveness from your biggest critic—you.

The honest truth is that the majority of men wear a mask to show the world that we are okay. But deep inside we are a mess! We battle daily with regrets, fears, doubts, and worries.

I was doing this very thing every day. I would wake up in the morning with an inner critic telling me I would be doing better if my parents hadn't died when I was young. From there I would move into an elaborate "What If" fantasy, recreating a make-believe scenario of having a wonderful upbringing with healthy and perfect parents. No one had problems in my fantasy and everything turned out just right.

In addition to telling me that my life would have been smooth sailing if my parents had lived longer, my inner critic liked to point out the many other disappointments I'd faced over the years, from getting into debt at the age of seventeen to not finishing college to not being satisfied in my career. I would journal those thoughts and list complaints about my life and create more "What If" situations.

In the morning, I would wake up with the same mindset, hoping for a different result. I wasn't looking inside myself. I fixated on others or my environment to show me my next step. I wasn't looking forward in my life and having a vision of the man I wanted to be. I was stuck between the past and present.

I regretted my past—the pain and disappointment it brought. I punished myself with thoughts of "I am not good enough." I emotionally recreated my trauma in a vicious cycle. I would fantasize that I had parents, a healthy childhood, and no lack of the material things that I wanted as a child. I even fantasized about being taller and more muscular than I was.

The world will never show you the truth of who you are.

I did not like the Javier inside of me. I would look at other people and see they were happy and satisfied, especially some of my religious peers, and I would rant in my head, "They are fakers! Look at them pretending to be happy just because they are children of God."

The truth is that God wants you to fully and unconditionally love yourself first. Why? If you don't, how can you love others in the same way? If you don't look for the good, the great, and the amazing in you, how can you look for it in others? If you don't praise and support yourself in a moment of struggle, how are you going to support others in a meaningful way?

I was living a lie inside myself. I was giving, but not receiving from the source. My Holy Father desperately wanted me to love myself every second of the day. He wanted me to learn to love myself fully so that I could move forward with the plan that He had for me. Jesus calls us to change the world but if we don't fully love ourselves, that fire inside will never light up.

Have no fears, doubts, or worries, as God is with you. Once we act from our faith in God, He will reveal his next step for us. We might not know His master plan, but we can trust that He will take care of the big picture. We grow to love ourselves as

He is loving us. We are His creation. There is no imperfection, and His love through us can change the world.

Once you allow love and compassion into your heart, you become powerful beyond belief. Love is life; love will conquer darkness and set you free. When you love yourself, you also allow others to be more compassionate with themselves. If you trust this process, you can change the world, starting with loving yourself.

Reflect on:

1) *What action can you do today to show your love for yourself?*

2) *When you look in the mirror at yourself, say, "I love you. I really love you." How does that feel? Can you look yourself in the eyes?*

3) *What are the proudest moments in your life? Share this with your partner.*

CHAPTER 2

Healing Childhood Wounds: Learning to Love Yourself

"Return, O faithless sons; I will hear your faithlessness. Behold, we come to you, for you are the Lord our God."

—Jeremiah 3:22 (ESV)

Your Past Does Not Determine Your Future

(CHRISTINA)

As a kid, I never felt I was good enough or attractive enough to succeed. I was not in the popular crowd and felt limited by the social hierarchy in school. The lack of diversity in my hometown and the push for material wealth clashed with my inner sense of self. I strived to prove my worth as I experimented with dressing from second-hand stores and listening to alternative music.

Even though I was raised Catholic, I never felt particularly close to God. I had moments of prayer as a little kid bargaining for the best outcome, but there was no real relationship there. It was one-sided, and it halted once I hit puberty. Unfortunately, that is when I needed Him the most.

I now know that I struggled with depression during adolescence. After dropping out of Catechism classes in the fourth grade, I went to Mass with my family on holidays, but my church life evaporated. Occasionally, I visited friends' youth groups and I went on a service trip to Appalachia one summer. Even so, I was not even aware of God's invitation in my life.

In high school, God became completely dormant. I stopped attending Mass completely, as did my family. Additionally, my grades never seemed good enough, my looks never seemed perfect enough, my waist never seemed slim enough. My political views differed from my father and we would get into arguments almost on a daily basis.

I was desperate to "fix" my situation and figured leaving the Midwest was the perfect escape plan. I was already over high school, plotting my escape by sophomore year.

Lost in the Wilderness of Past Relationships

(CHRISTINA)

In college, I rebooted my self-image by making new friends, re-conceptualized my own beauty by finding my own sense of style. I began to believe in my own intellect only to then get involved in an emotionally abusive relationship for two years. A toxic detour. I completely lost myself and my goals. My boyfriend criticized my appearance, my academic interests, and my friends. His words cut down my self-confidence. He refused to commit to our relationship, yet would also not completely let me go—pursuing me, then dumping me, then pursuing me again.

I worked at a cafe that was the social center in our college town. My on-and-off boyfriend would "punish" me when we were broken up by bringing in his dates and flaunting his new prospects. When he wasn't dating someone, he would harass me at work by showing up to stare or stalk, throwing off my equilibrium and sense of safety.

This intensified when I decided to study abroad in Spain my junior year of college. My decision and independence terrified him. He lashed out even harder by refusing to talk to me for periods of time, then ridiculing my choice of major (sociology) and plan to study in Spain, a country he considered "the third world."

While I was abroad, after a long and tortuous year of emotional mind games and manipulation, I broke free. I returned to campus with a packed class schedule, determined to graduate in my fourth year while working part-time. I put blinders on and started again with a new group of friends. I cut my long curly hair and swore off dating. He did show up unannounced (again) at my job right before I graduated. I told him that I didn't believe in romantic love and walked away. I wanted nothing to do with him.

Even though I'd broken free from the abusive relationship, I hadn't quite recovered. I still felt vulnerable and unattractive.

I couldn't see myself as worthy to have a partner who treated me kindly and with respect. And I still felt that something better, something that would fix me and make me feel beautiful and interesting, was right around the corner. Somewhere else.

I also still equated being in a relationship with being valuable in society. No matter my academic comeback and success, no matter my tough talk about not believing in romantic love, no matter my friendships and platonic relationships, I could not shake this formula. I compared myself relentlessly to my sister who dated the same boy since she was fifteen, happy and secure in her relationship. Next to her, I felt like a total and utter failure. She had succeeded easily at something that always seemed to elude me.

Four days after graduating from college, I bolted for New York City in a U-Haul with a friend. After a desperate job search, I became a foster care social worker in a Catholic non-profit agency. I was surrounded by nuns who defied stereotype, believed in social justice, and asked me almost monthly when I was going to get married. I desperately wanted to get married, but I secretly feared that I was not good enough.

My feelings of insufficiency still lingered and my escape to NYC proved lonely, economically challenging, and emotionally harsh. I worked in neighborhoods stricken with generational poverty and did home visits in tandem with other colleagues who were burnt out and trying to get out of social service as soon as possible. I stopped dating for five years and focused instead on getting a better job so I could live alone and then attend graduate school in peace.

"Belief in oneself is required for healing."
—Caroline Myss

I ended up getting a full scholarship to Columbia University to get my Master's in Social Work. This was a huge win. My education fueled my love for learning and passion for social justice. Those two years were a bright spot in my personal development and gave me a sense of deep accomplishment and fulfillment. Although I didn't know it at the time, God was watching out for me and helping me prepare for the future.

The Only Person You Need to Save Is Yourself

(CHRISTINA)

Regardless of my personal accomplishments, I continued to struggle with my own feelings of inadequacy. I had made a career of rescuing others when I still hadn't learned to save myself. I didn't even realize I needed to! A wounded healer, my brokenness led to many moments of loneliness, weight gain, self-loathing, and isolation. In addition, I still felt I needed a marital relationship to complete me. I felt inadequate because I wasn't dating, let alone married.

Why wasn't I with someone?! What was wrong with me? (A killer book on this is *There is Nothing Wrong with You* by Cheri Huber.)

During grad school, I would go in and out of hope. I had no idea how much God was waiting to help me. I was in a self-imposed wilderness and couldn't look up. Dipping in and out of churches, I longed for a spiritual hook. There was an invitation, but I was not fully listening, and I certainly missed the signs.

After leaving work one day, I was "jumped" by two teenagers. I remember feeling anger before passing them—frustration and fatigue about my life. I had just come from the ER with a suicidal student for the second day in a row. I was burnt, broken, and lost.

The young men tried to take my purse off my shoulder, and I instantly fought back, screaming. To this day, I have no idea where my primal rage came from at that moment. I never yielded…and kept my purse.

Something instantly changed in me. I had exploded with outrage, indignation, and obscenities that I did not know I had in my vocabulary. The attack was a cosmic brick. I woke up determined to change my life. I refused to be a victim.

Life Changes When Your Mind Changes

(CHRISTINA)

After seeking therapy and cleaning up my diet, I began to get reacquainted with God and feel him in my life again. Around this time, I started visiting my sister in San Francisco. There, I envisioned a new life and planned to leave NYC to move to the Bay Area. I had just ended another dead-end relationship and was hungry to start anew. I quickly got a second job part-time to save money to move west.

I applied for five jobs in and around San Francisco and received five job offers. Even though I rebounded into another unhealthy relationship, I stayed on my course to move across the country and plotted ahead. No matter the pain and discomfort, I did not give up. I had to believe that is was God guiding me.

Upon arriving in the Bay Area, something inside me burned for something more. My sister told me on the day that I arrived that she and her husband were moving in a year to Arizona. My "safety net" of having family nearby instantly dissolved. This immediate disappointment woke me up and deep loneliness reawakened. I was alone. Again.

From there, depression and frequent crying jags filled my days. Even though I was thriving in my new job, I felt scared and alone. This sadness propelled me to hunt for meaning in my life. I found a spiritual community and a church. Every Sunday, I was around people who loved me. I gave back to the church. I volunteered. I served. A big piece of my heart filled. A spiritual and emotional renaissance began. I felt like God's child, I allowed his grace to fill my imperfections, and I began to shine.

You Are Good Enough

(CHRISTINA)

I had a messy ride, but it was uniquely my own. It led me to God and my perfect partner. It was only when I saw my imperfections as part of a divine plan that I could fully surrender.

My husband, Javier, came into my life when I was whole, not in my humanity, but in my love for God. I knew that He had me covered. God's plan was better than mine. I took to heart the phrase "Thy will be done." I knew that even if I didn't find a spouse, I was still good enough with God at my side. I could lead a fulfilling and worthwhile life. Even alone, I knew that I had value, that I was enough. At this point in my life, I began to pray to surrender my search for a perfect match to Him.

As soon as I "let go and let God," things fell into place. I was 33 years old, content in my career and my relationship with God. My good friend from work, Sheila, invited me to meet her husband's (Luis), best friend from middle school. After many months of trying to schedule time, we planned a dinner date at their house. That was the evening that I met Javier. It was magical.

Our childhood wounds and adulthood failures are gifts from God. They lead us to heal and drive us to look inward. I cannot deny the periods of self-doubt, inadequacy, or insecurity. But, I can choose to embrace my humanity as His daughter. God loves me and you to no end.

Healing Childhood Wounds: Learning to Overcome Loneliness and Abuse

(JAVIER)

As a child, I grew up instructed by my father to forget the past. No matter what happened—either good or bad, he told me to forget it and move on. I carried that for decades of my life without realizing that although it is good to forget, it is necessary to heal first.

My father never shared or spoke about my mother. He did not introduce me to his memories of her in our conversations—only telling me that she loved me and that she named me Javier. The rest he suggested to forget and move on.

The more I asked "why" about being put into an orphanage, the less my father would explain. Not being able to talk about what happened added unnecessary pain. Why did I go through such horrible abuse in a religious environment? His simple answer was, "Forget about it. Move on."

My brother took the same approach when dealing with my father's death. When I arrived in San Jose, California to live with him, there was no conversation. I would sob with grief every time I was in the shower over missing my father and mother. My brother answered the same as my father, "Forget it and move on."

∼

My younger years were filled with back-to-back trauma. When people would ask about my childhood, I opened with, "My mom died when I was two years old." It went downhill from there. I was born in Madrid, Spain, and my mother died of pancreatic cancer. She was diagnosed when she was pregnant with me; it was a miracle that I was born. I was a "surprise," and my next closest sibling in age is eleven years older than me.

Raised without a mother, I often felt lonely and abandoned. My siblings—who were much older than me—left me to find their own ways. And, although my father loved me and often showed me this, he had gone through many health problems and his own emotional trauma. This meant that at periods of my childhood I was emotionally abused by him and neglected.

At age seven, I was put in an orphanage by force and physically and verbally abused by the priest and nuns who ran the orphanage. I felt abandoned and rejected growing up. My childhood was so painful that my stomach still turns and twists when I think about it.

While fighting against Franco in the Spanish Civil War, my father was imprisoned as a prisoner of war (POW). He contracted tuberculosis and suffered multiple related illnesses during his mid-twenties, which caused him to lose a lung. Due to this, his left lung grew bigger and put pressure on his heart, and he suffered several heart attacks. He developed a tumor on his remaining lung. Liquid would form around this lung, so he would have to drain it every day through a tube that came out from his armpit for drainage.

Every day he would make me watch him clean his wound and drain liquid from that tube. I couldn't stand it at first; I was afraid and felt so sad for my dad. Some days, the smell and his painful expression made me vomit. His reasoning was that by watching, I would be a tougher man in life.

Although my father loved me and tried in his way to show it, he was never empowering with his words. When I was a child, he would tell me that I would never amount to more than a pimp or a bouncer in a nightclub. The constant verbal abuse from him diluted my childhood dreams.

Whenever my dad was in the hospital and I felt abandoned, I wished that I had a picture of my mom with me so I could pour my heart out to her, but I didn't. According to my siblings, she decided not to take photos with me because she looked devastated by pancreatic cancer. I grew up always imagining how she was around me. Did she kiss me a lot or hug me? What kind of words did she say to me? What was she thinking when she was holding me? What were her feelings for me?

I recreated the answers to these questions in my mind by piecing together stories from my siblings and people who knew her as a Band-Aid for the much deeper wounds of my emotional abuse and neglect. All the cumulative rejection of my childhood and verbal abuse from my father and the horrible experience from the orphanage were too much for my mind and heart to take.

By my mid-twenties, I started to realize the many ways it had affected me. One of the biggest was in my dating life; it wasn't healthy. There was a lot of drama...and relationships with baggage. I was lost and looking for comfort. My thirst for a motherly love resulted in very irrational behavior such as angry outbursts, ignoring or not returning girlfriends' phone calls, and dating more than one person at a time. I was broken and suffering inside.

I Am a Motherless Child

(JAVIER)

I love the song by John Legend called "Motherless Child." It resonates with me because it reminds me of feeling so alone as a child. I often felt lost early in life as I did not have a mom waiting for me at home or a consistent force of compassion in my life. In fact, it took me years to actually identify what I was missing.

I internalized and experienced men as primary caregivers in my childhood. My "parents" were my dad and later my brother who was eleven years older than me. I received tough, stoic, fatherly love, but there was no maternal love. After my father's death, I was not encouraged to grieve or share my feelings. I longed for a mom and a gentle hand.

My father passed away when I was thirteen. Three years after his death, during my teenage years, I broke down in tears every time I faced struggles or rejection. I would sob uncontrollably without knowing exactly why. None of my dating relationships lasted more than three months. In my heart, I had a dreaded feeling that I was not accepted.

Later on, I realized how much a soft touch, a hug, and words of encouragement are necessary for a healthy childhood. No wonder I now love interacting with kids so much. What I didn't get from my mother, I now give to others.

Once I realized what I was missing, I did not take action and seek professional counseling or help. Being tough was more important and "figuring it out on my own" was part of manhood.

> ## *"If you don't heal the wounds of childhood, you bleed into the future."*
>
> ## —OPRAH WINFREY

My life went from trauma to drama. I was just going with the flow. My relationships were like missed connections that often escalated to arguments and silent treatments, lacking intimacy and emotional safety. This was not due to the women I dated. I was a broken man, hollow on the inside. And I had abandoned myself in the process.

One Bad Relationship after Another

(JAVIER)

The less we love who we are, the less we think we deserve in life. God provides more than enough love for us. Yet, unless we value who we are as a child of God, we will settle for less. If you think of yourself as unworthy and undeserving, you will not see God's plan for you.

∾

In my late twenties, I found myself engaged to a woman I was not in love with. I was living a lie and depending on this woman to fill a hole she never could, taking both of us down in the process.

Something inside me snapped. I had to stop the madness. I walked away from the train wreck of that relationship, leaving everything except a futon behind. That said, not all my relationships were horrible. Some of them I neglected because of my pain. I ended up emotionally investing more in bad relationships because they mirrored my hurt inside. Thankfully, I recognized this pattern, and I realized that I was reliving my past trauma in my relationships. It was me who needed major remodeling. I needed to find peace to go inside and the face the mess.

I never realized how important it is to check and balance the experiences in your life. There are good experiences and bad experiences that I tended to just forget. But in reality, I didn't forget the bad ones. I just kept them underground and did not deal with them. With this last dismantled relationship, I realized it was time to change.

Love is an intense feeling that can bring people to ecstasy or to their lowest common denominator in life. In my relationships, I sought a feeling of euphoria that would create a sense of belonging and serve as my substitute for maternal love. I searched for someone to always be there and comfort me when things went wrong.

I never stopped to really evaluate my relationships. Though I believed deeply in Christ, I shied away from that topic with all the women I dated. I was always seeking a magic formula that would bring me all the motherly love that I needed in life—always wanting and longing, but never bringing the best version of myself to the relationship.

In a moment of grace, which I now believe came from God, I realized I needed to fill my emotional tank. I needed to find a higher purpose for being with someone instead of for the sole sake of fixing my childhood wounds. Instead, I needed someone who I would celebrate and cherish. This relationship would be founded on unconditional love.

I got my own apartment, jetted to IKEA, bought all my furniture on credit, and assembled it in one night. It was exhilarating, terrifying, and amazing. In the wee hours of this all-nighter, I remember sitting in my mini-man cave feeling overwhelmed with peace for the first time in years. I was finally coming home and ready to work on myself.

Knowing that I needed to get my finances under control, I gave up my car, my beloved pet—everything I had known—to start fresh. It was incredibly painful to leave everything that I knew for many years, but it had to be done. I created a turning point, a new life, by letting go. By loving myself, I shut down the noise of self-loathing, opening a path to returning to God in my life.

$\sim$

When I met Christina, my life went from a foggy dawn to pure beach sunshine. I felt I was traveling from London in winter to the sunny Bahamas with a cocktail in my hand. I ended up just staring at the beautiful beach surrounded by palm trees.

She was the poster girl I put on my bedroom wall when I was thirteen years old. On top of that, she was a Capricorn. She was my horoscope compatible sign I have been searching for. (Yes, I love that stuff!)

Our courtship was nothing like I had experienced before. It was surreal and meant to be. I was enamored with Christina's every move. She was independent and creating social change in the world. Coming from a tech environment, I thought this was very attractive. Christina had a strong character and didn't take nonsense from anyone. She was full of life and also broken inside. The thing that won me over was Christina's big heart.

My dream was to marry someone who was in the faith, but I was always embarrassed to ask my past relationships if they believed in God. In fact, I never attended any religious services with a single one of them. That was a sign that I deeply regret ignoring. But Christina was in love with Jesus Christ, and she swept me in.

True Love Brings up All Your Emotions

(JAVIER)

Once Christina came into my life, my childhood wounds resurfaced more intensely. The good, the bad, and the ugly were right there, not moving. Since I was falling in love with Christina deeply, I felt extremely vulnerable and weak. The same destructive behaviors of anger and verbal abuse I had demonstrated in other relationships started up again with even more intensity.

From there, I began playing mind games: "Do you love me?" "I don't love you." I ignored her to make her feel guilty with an attitude of "show me what you got." I burst into tears at times because I feared being abandoned and neglected again. I was completely overwhelmed and could not express my emotions with any words. I would get angry at little things. If she took a phone call while we were out, I would snap and call off the night.

I was scared. How could this be happening? I felt unconditional love for the first time in my life. But instead of it leading to blissful love, it seemed that it only led to angry outbursts. I relived my feelings of being abandoned. The more this continued, the more I damaged myself and my amazing relationship with Christina. And I couldn't figure out why.

Revisiting the Past

(JAVIER)

As I struggled to heal myself and save my relationship with Christina, I was forced to dig back into my past. I had many unresolved issues with my family, my religion, and myself.

$\sim$

My father left this world when I was thirteen years old. Two weeks after his death, I flew to the United States to live with my next closest sibling who was eleven years my senior. My brother, Miguel, became my legal guardian at age twenty-four. He was living in California with his girlfriend and her family.

Despite his struggles, while raising me, my father is my hero. I loved him deeply. I can still smell his essence and the tingly feeling of his mustache when he kissed me as a child. His soft hands, his strong, empowering look, his charisma, and his love for life.

I miss him every day. But during his life, he went through many struggles. They affected him deeply, causing emotional unsteadiness, and sometimes even hardness. He survived tuberculosis at a young age but lost one of his lungs. An illness marked him throughout his life. Even so, he became a Spanish Civil War veteran, experiencing time as a prisoner of war.

He was a gentleman, and I am not embarrassed or ashamed to share this. Growing up with him, I observed how he was around women. He was extremely polite, a great listener, romantic, and charismatic.

I remember one Saturday afternoon, there was heavy rain when we were in downtown Madrid. A lady passed next to us, and my father noticed that she was getting wet. Since she didn't have an umbrella, he immediately took his long coat and used it to cover her. He insisted that a beautiful woman like her should not get wet in the rain. We accompanied her to where she was going. I observed the entire interaction and fell in love with the way my father spoke to women. Always with respect, admiration, and humor.

This was a gift my father left for me to use in creating future relationships.

Unfortunately, in addition to his chivalry, he also had a terrible temper and spent his life battling many emotional demons from the past. The fire that fueled his courage with his illness, charisma, and intelligence also brought fits of rage, paranoia, and mistrust of others. His defense mechanism was to unleash anger or verbal abuse and create big scenes in public.

One powerful memory of my father stays with me. We lived in a big flat in a suburb of Madrid, called Carabanchel. Our flat was on the third floor and this building had no elevator since it was built in the 1960s.

One afternoon, my Dad and I were heading upstairs to our flat when our neighbor was coming downstairs. As we passed one another, my father happily greeted him with "Buenos Dias!" The man didn't reply or acknowledge my father. My father's face twisted into a rage. He immediately chased the man downstairs. When the man glanced at my father, my father slapped him hard in the face. "Don't you ever ignore me in front of my son," my father commanded.

I idolized my father as a kid. He was untouchable in my eyes. Was it right what he did? At the time, it didn't bother me, but as a grown man and father, I would not want my kids to have this memory of me.

My dad had a turbulent upbringing as well. He never spoke well of my grandfather even though he, too, was part of the Civil War in Spain and fought against the fascists. The only story that my dad would share often is that my grandfather learned how to read and write during the Civil War from a Russian soldier. The only other information I knew about my grandfather was that he was a stone carver for tombstones. He made the tombstone of Pablo Iglesias Posse, the Socialist Union leader during the Civil War. That's where my father got the majority of his political and religious beliefs. Beyond that, he never shared anything more.

My guess was that my dad never had a good relationship with his own father and that led to a constant struggle with his own family. He would tell me stories of fighting to get food or work during the war. My father shared the story of how his father almost killed someone who was trying to rip off one of my aunts.

As a child, I witnessed more than one episode of my father's fury. He had horrible road rage when driving his car, as well as endless arguments with fellow spectators when watching Real Madrid soccer matches. I remember my father feeling embarrassed and infuriated in restaurants because he thought people were making fun of him. I even recollect him pulling a knife on a neighbor who had mocked his medical condition and embarrassed him at a coffee shop.

My father verbally abused his second wife and broke personal property in front of my eyes. Sometimes he frightened me to the point that just a look would terrify me. The cycle of rage would calm for a short week and then it would happen again out of the blue. One unexpected quiet dinner moment could explode into a snap of anger.

This alone would have set me up for turbulence in future relationships. Habits learned from my father were affecting the way I dealt with Christina during our courtship. But my childhood had left me with even deeper wounds and, in addition to learning how to treat romantic relationships, I also had to learn how to trust.

The Orphanage

(JAVIER)

When I look back at my childhood, there were several factors that led to my struggles with vulnerability and trust. But one experience stands out as damaging to both my heart and my faith.

One day, out of the blue, I was sent to a "summer camp" in the southern part of Madrid. I was seven years old. My dad was very sick that summer. I remember the lady that my dad married calling my older brother for help to take my dad to the emergency room. I also remember my siblings discussing what they were going to do with me while Dad was in the hospital.

I thought that I was being sent to a camp to spend time with a new bunch of kids and was excited about activities outside of my environment. I soon realized that many of the children had no parents. Some of them acted very strange—not like the kids that I knew. There were lots of fights, personal items missing, verbal and physical abuse from the staff, especially the clergy who ran the camp.

Soon enough, I realized that the "camp" was an orphanage. My world flipped upside down. Rather than making new friends, I spent my time trying to hold on to my personal items and to avoid abuse. I cannot begin to convey the complete loneliness and sadness I felt there. It was like I didn't matter. At age seven, I could not understand why I was there. It was dark, scary, cold, and I couldn't make sense of it.

All the kids wore the same clothing at the orphanage. As a welcome package, you got two of everything. Two pairs of pants, two pairs of underwear, two pairs of socks, two sweaters, two T-shirts, and one pair of boots. The trick was to keep them from getting stolen.

The clothing that was given to us was handed down from previous kids. You could clearly see the previous name crossed off. Some garments had no more space from where the former owners had put their initials. But it didn't matter. Even if you wrote your name big on your clothes or hid them under your mattress, they would most likely be stolen by other children.

Personal property in the orphanage was what you carried with you at that moment, not what you stored under your bed or in a secret hiding place. The items that you carried were the only things that belonged to you for sure at the time. Personal items were free to all and at risk of being stolen.

But that wasn't the worst of it. Horrible things happened in that orphanage, things that I wouldn't wish upon anyone.

Children were sexually and psychologically abused by both peers and clergy leaders. We experienced scarcity, specifically with food and clothing, which created a prison-like atmosphere. I felt that I couldn't escape, but held on to the false hope that this nightmare would be over when I left the orphanage, and that one day I could just forget it happened.

That day did not arrive. At the orphanage, Sundays were the loneliest. I would spend the weekends there while some of the kids would leave to stay with relatives. They would come back from their weekend all happy with full bags of candy and treats. I had so much envy and jealousy.

Taking a shower was like a scene from a prison camp. We lined up with torn pajamas in our arms waiting to take a shower. No shower curtain, no privacy—just a water pipe from the ceiling and the kid behind you pushing you so you wouldn't take more than two minutes.

Even the moments of fun we allowed ourselves could be dangerous. Sometimes, as most kids do, we fooled around jumping from bed to bed, or getting into fights, or stealing the cheap art paints from the classroom, or even making funny penis drawings on the windows. This bonded us sometimes, though we would pray that the nuns didn't catch us in the act.

If we got caught, the nuns would use their rosary beads to whip us in the back. Rosary beads were made of a very durable material. The worst part was feeling the scratches of the metal cross of the rosary on your back.

Having few possessions and being beaten by the nuns, however, was not the worst thing we suffered. That came at night. The dorm room was full of life before the lights went out. You could hear laughter, kids playing around, and jokes. In a way, we had a sense of brotherhood.

However, as soon as the lights went out and the night shift counselor made the final walk, the abuse began. The kids who were fifteen and up were the ones who took advantage of the younger kids. The orphanage had separate rooms from ages five to ten and from ten to seventeen. In the ten to seventeen-year-old room, older kids sexually abused the younger ones.

You could hear the older kids, the sex predators, jumping into other kids' beds covering their mouths, undressing them and raping them. They worked as a team. Three to four of the older kids would tag team and abuse a younger child together.

Once in a while, you would hear cries for help, but the rule was to turn to your other side and try to fall asleep. In the morning, you could easily identify the victims. Their heads looking down with bruises on their bodies and dried tears on the faces. It felt like the boogie man appearing at night. And just like the boogie man, it seemed there was no escape.

The key to survival in the orphanage was to belong to a gang. This way, you could keep all your possessions and avoid rape or getting beaten up. The hope for me was to make it to seventeen years old and run away like most of the kids did. (Many of them went to juvenile hall and wrote to me years later.) So I joined the gang that would protect me and my possessions. We were a group who watched each others' backs, lied, and even comforted one another.

The membership fee to join the gang was to steal anything at any minute during the day, beat up anyone at any given point, and keep your mouth shut about anything that was going on in the gang. Our gang leader made a lot of visits to the separate residence where the priests lived. We suspected that our leader was sexually abused by one of the priests, but nothing was ever said.

And that was the safest place I could be—in that gang.

One day, my sister, Alicia, came to visit me. I remember I met her in the lobby of the orphanage, which had marble floor and 1970s furniture. She brought me Dopey the dwarf from the Disney movie *Snow White*.

I was so brainwashed by the mental and physical abuse that even though I had seen her a year earlier, I couldn't recognize her. To try to help me remember, she kept asking me questions, but it didn't help. I was so hurt, disturbed, and scared that I left her in the lobby. She was crying her eyes out as I held a toy that eventually got stolen the same day.

My prayers for an escape were answered unexpectedly and earlier than I had hoped. I got chickenpox and spent several weeks in the infirmary of the orphanage. My father was contacted and began the process of removing me from the orphanage in order to take me home.

Despite the fact that I was in the infirmary to recover from my illness, I was still mistreated by the clergy. We were left unsupervised with nothing to do. Some of the children would feel better and want to play. But if we played or got out of bed, the nuns would come in and beat the children with rosaries. The infirmary was the last stop on my journey in that horrible place. The chickenpox and the marks on my back and legs were evidence of my illness and served as my ticket home.

During my time in the infirmary, my perception of the clergy changed from holy to damaged. They were erratic, mean, and abusive. Many of the men and women were hiding their pain with the mask of religion.

Sometimes I wondered why I wasn't able to contact my dad while I was at the orphanage. Thanks to getting sick, I was able to go home. But if that hadn't happened, I would have had no way to communicate with my family. We were treated like prisoners with no right to communicate with the outside world.

When my father was notified, apparently his heart was broken. Perhaps he was feeling better or perhaps he realized that he needed to confront the issue of having a younger son who most desperately needed his love and protection. I know that as soon as he saw me, he felt horrible. I still remember his watery eyes when he picked me up from the orphanage. When I returned home, I did not enter my own bedroom, and I referred to my father as "sir." This hurt him, too, and it was many months before we became more comfortable with each other again.

When I left the orphanage, I thought that my nightmare would be over. In a literal way, it was. I never experienced abuse like that again. And yet, those memories still haunt me every day. This and the death of my parents are wounds that I am still healing from.

∾

At the time I met Christina, these memories had been buried deep for many years and I had not dealt with them. Before I could fully connect with and love her, I had to find a way to heal myself and begin to recover from my past.

Fortunately, before I met Christina, I had begun my walk back to God. I had begun the hard work of finding meaning, strength, and God's grace in the experiences of my life—good and bad.

As I struggled to heal my relationship with Christina, I was confronted with the demons of my past and forced to face them. Over the years, in developing a relationship with God, I learned that the only way out of the prison of the past is to accept myself unconditionally. This doesn't mean I stopped trying to heal and change. Rather, I had to make peace with the past, feeling the pain to fully live in the present and create a new now. There is no way around the emotions. I had to go through them to unlock their hold on me.

My childhood wounds still arise, but I am aware of their purpose. I love myself and embrace the good of my dark childhood. I also acknowledge that it does not own me. During my courtship with Christina, I experienced many triggers that shot off hidden memories from the past. These memories still held power, and my shame around them took a toll on my courtship and later on my marriage.

As I confronted my past, I was gradually able to stop sabotaging my relationship with Christina. I was able to love her and to let her love me. However, it wasn't a one-shot deal. The pain from my childhood is something that I still confront. Even now, I continually work to progress in my healing process.

Making Peace with the Past

(JAVIER)

Growing up, my family history was so painful that I would spend hours fantasizing that my life was perfect. I would pretend that my parents never passed away, but that I still came to America to study with my brother. I focused on how I would feel if things were more "normal."

I would do this again and again. To my surprise, nothing changed. I was still the same person with the same pain. I didn't realize this habit until much later in my life.

Instead of reimagining your past, create your future.

 ∽

When you forgive your past, it empowers you to purify your heart and heal yourself. This is extremely valuable as you enter into a lifetime commitment of partnership. Let the triggers come up. Be an open book. Share, cry, and celebrate with your significant other.

My triggers of abandonment and fear of rejection formed during my childhood. The verbal and mental abuse from my father and the time that I spent in the orphanage fueled them, and they would pop up when I became vulnerable. The most painful trigger of all was the absence of motherly love that I was so desperately and blindly looking for through my mid-twenties and early thirties.

The Lord brings us to this world brand new, with the purest hearts of all, with the gifts, talents, and the potential to be free and be a part of Him. As we grow in life, the wrong information is given to us either by life or circumstances beyond our control.

Your narrative is not who you are. The negative circumstances that created scars are not who you are. Don't believe the lies of the past. Anything is possible, and your marriage can be a testimony to that truth.

I look back at my past and, as painful it can be, I see the gifts I received. I do not have a photo of my mother and me together from my childhood. This was very difficult for me to accept. With God's grace, I now know that she is all around me.

When my anger bubbles up and wants to unleash, I take a step back and sit with the discomfort. Sometimes, doing nothing is the best response so I can let the feeling pass through my body.

I pause inside myself and reflect before I act. I do not want to derail my relationship with my wife and kids by acting out destructive behaviors. The past no longer determines my choices. I see the cycle, and I can stop it.

Despite the early loss of my parents, I would not want it any other way. I was an orphan and I left a country by myself at thirteen. This is a valuable part of my story and it has brought strength, resilience, and my faith in God.

I embrace my past because it informs me, teaches, and leads me to my faith, making me stronger than most. I don't let my childhood wounds dictate what God has for me in my marriage. I am writing a new story in my life.

Reflect on:

1) Does your fiancé or partner know about your childhood? Is there anything you feel compelled to share with her/him to build trust and intimacy in your relationship?

2) What ways today do you feel that your childhood affects how you seek and receive love in your relationship?

3) How can your past experiences in childhood inform and strengthen your relationship with your fiancé/partner?

CHAPTER 3

Healthy Boundaries

"As for a person who stirs up division,
after warning him once and then twice,
have nothing more to do with him."

—Titus 3:10 (ESV)

Learning to Say No to Say Yes

(CHRISTINA)

Even though I am stubborn and fiery by nature, I struggled with the "disease to please others" most of my life. This came from a need to be liked and accepted even at my own expense. It was part socialization, part personality, and part coping mechanism. But it backfired, again and again, causing frustration and resentment. This reflex to ignore my true desires, needs, and even God's voice clouded my judgment. I often said "Yes" when I knew in my heart that "No" was the right answer.

My journey of self-love and self-acceptance intertwines with my faith as well as a steep learning curve with setting boundaries—learning to love myself enough to say no, stick with it, and believe that I'm worth it.

I am not ashamed of all the self-affirmations posted on my mirror and all the prayer slips in my wallet and purse. I need daily reminders that I am loved by God.

If you don't prioritize your physical, mental, and spiritual health, you'll be lucky if someone stops you.

I remember my first boss calling me out when I was working through lunch. "Stop that right now!" Terrified by her authority, my stomach sunk as I thought that I was in trouble.

She met my eyes and calmly stated, "You don't get paid for lunch. So take it." I sat in silence. "Get the hell out of here because this work will eat you up. Bye!"

She turned abruptly and whisked away onto the elevator. I quickly followed with my half-eaten sandwich. I never stopped taking a lunch break from then on. I would go outside, sit in the nearby courtyard, people watch, and sit in silence.

Taking lunch was actually a big deal. It was my first brush with self-care, and I'm grateful to that boss for teaching it to me. Often, if we don't make our health a priority, no one will stop us. And our jobs will take and take and spit us out if we let them.

American culture prides itself on being busy—always on the go, working hard at the cost of one's health, family time, sleep, face-to-face conversations, and sanity. Ask people in your life, "How are you?" At least in Silicon Valley, the most common response is, "Oh, my gosh. I am so busy." Where does self-care come into play if we barely sleep or eat?

Even as children, we are endlessly pressured to prove ourselves: get good grades, excel in sports, get accepted into a good college, nail a great job. As adults we're expected to make the most of that "great job" and then move up from position to position, no matter the personal cost. It's a never-ending trap.

When did saying "No" begin to feel like a crime? It's actually a healthy behavior and keeps relationships intact. Learning to say "No" is also key to having healthy boundaries. If we are overscheduled, overworked, and overstressed, it is even more vital that we can draw a line in the sand at times and say "No" to take care of ourselves, succeed at what we really want to do or just recuperate from life.

When do we value ourselves for being human in the midst of our failures and brokenness? When do we go beyond the to-do list and look at whether we are really fulfilled in our lives? When do we sit in silence or just do nothing?

Give Yourself to God

(CHRISTINA)

Life is fickle, full of change, and unpredictable. Our path is often unclear.

So many times, it is easier to just get through the day, mindlessly following the daily routine and overscheduling ourselves.

Letting go of control is our biggest fear because there are so many unanswered questions and variables in life. So much of my life has been learning how to surrender and trust the process. God is doing the battling for me, and I really don't have to micromanage his role in my life.

Am I following my gut, God's word? Am I on the right track or am I going nowhere? Am I operating out of ego? So much doubt and self-judgment persist.

Any success by society's standards will give out, expire, or evaporate over time. All things lose their shine, including the optimal circumstances. We need something more in life and something more to ground our marriage throughout our lives.

We are living in a temporal time and our lives belong to God. He chooses when we go, how we go. Our challenge is to be here now, make something of our lives, and find meaning in the midst of the hot mess.

Getting ready for marriage is committing to a partner who gets that the game is rigged against you in the material world, that basing a union on faith is the closest way to building a foundation from rock—God being the only constant you can count on.

Real life will break you down. Failure is inevitable and happens every day. The only way to love yourself is to embrace your heart and have the strength to not buckle to the pressures of the outside world.

Don't give your power to anyone or anything to complete you—just give your relationship up to God. This is the best start for any partnership.

God is your ally, your truth-teller, and your secret sauce when the material world tells you lies. Your faith is your backbone when the world won't let up and you can't look up or stand up. When you identify with the world, you take on its endless suffering, misery, injustice, and pain. When you hold onto God, you live by what really matters the most.

When you go to your spiritual source, God shows you that there is a bigger picture, more meaning than meets the eye, and that who you are is not determined by your environment. Don't buy that story. You are not my social media handle; You are bigger than that.

Internalizing your self-worth and value can seriously rock your world, including your most intimate relationships. God calls us to Him in self-forgiveness and self-acceptance.

As you accept yourself and become aware of your needs, you learn to discern what is right for you, which is not based on what you were taught or shown as a child. This may mean challenging childhood traditions or norms—what has been expected of you for years, if not generations.

Find Your tribe

(CHRISTINA)

Not all families of origin are created equal. That's part of life's diversity. Some of us are super close from birth, others grow close over time. Consider yourself blessed if this is the case. Not all of us are loved by those who gave birth to us. You cannot force people to support you, change, or behave the way you would like. This realization is key to your mental health and the sanctity of your marriage.

If you are not feeling the love from family, you need to figure out their role in your upcoming marriage—sooner rather than later. Don't set up your new bride or groom for family drama when it can be avoided by implementing healthy boundaries during your engagement.

The foundation you set about who spends time with you, attends your special day and gets access to your daily life needs to have a shortlist. You get to create a new union and that means no one gets a backstage pass without earning it.

Part of adulting is getting to choose your tribe, your community, your circle of people and influencers in your life. Marriage is about doing that with your partner for life.

You do not want to squander this self-reflection and access on folks who are negative and/or unsupportive of your choices and especially your partner. You create your world; it is not just given to you. If someone stirs the pot just to mess up the kitchen, you need to shut down the burner. No smoke, no fire.

$\sim$

Javi and I took a long, hard look at the people in our lives before we sauntered down the aisle. God brought people into our lives for a reason and He took them out in a heartbeat if needed. You need to watch, listen, reflect, and confer with your partner.

Do we want to do holidays with family? Where and how? Do we want to make our church a priority in our social life? Do we want to let go of some relationships that we were hanging onto out of guilt or tradition?

The answers to these questions may change over time. How you spend your holidays as a couple may shift with time, location, stage of your life. The key question is: are you spending it the best way for your marriage?

Listen to your heart. Choose to be with those who lift you up and bring out the best in you. Choose people who are there for the long haul, who have no hidden agenda, who will love you without strings attached. They will be the ones to support your marriage.

There will be a time when you will collapse or lose faith or feel diminished and can't fight for your marriage. The "D" word may be spoken or linger or tempt your thoughts. It's part of being human; we all fail and spiral and act out.

In the darkest moment of our marriage, I met with a divorce lawyer. I was broken, lost, and trapped in fear. In my heart, it felt like an out-of-body experience. I would ask myself, "Why am I pursuing the potential of divorce?" The answer was simple: I was going through the motions in a trance of fear.

Who will be there to have your back and fight for you? Who will hold up your marriage while you lie flat-lined on the ground? Who will tell you to slow down, breathe, and pray? You need this person or people because sometimes we cannot be there for ourselves.

These people are the prayer warriors in your life. They are your tribe who will hold your faith strong, so when you get back up, you can wipe yourself off and get your hair right.

If people in your life are not bringing you up now, look at that. They will not change; only God can change them. So limit their access to bringing you down. Take a look; you need to be selective about who you let into your married life.

When I moved to San Francisco from NYC, I was determined to do a life makeover. I was in the process of breaking free from negative, dysfunctional relationships and starting fresh. I was eager to reinvent myself, dive into the spiritual life, and reconcile my brokenness. I was ready to face my depression head-on while also joining a church.

On the first day in San Francisco, I arrived at my sister's home. She told me that she and her husband were planning on moving to Arizona. What a disappointment! It was the beginning of learning to trust and rely on God. Even family is limited as a safety net. Ultimately, it was just poor timing, but it served as a big lesson on leaning on God first.

Even our family of origin cannot fill our spiritual void or be our safety blanket. My expectations were clearly rewritten. I learned to go deeper to find peace from God and recognize the limitations of family.

We teach people how to treat us and setting healthy boundaries is the first step of this truism. If you cannot say "No," your "Yes" is meaningless. If you want to find your spiritual partner for life, you need to build credibility with yourself first.

I participated in many self-development seminars, and I remember distinctly being challenged to look at myself naked in the mirror and ponder how I felt about myself. Do I love my stretch-marked, muffin-topped body and all? Do I see my true beauty and forgive my cosmetic faults? Can I look at myself in the eyes? Do I treat myself like my own BFF and truly enjoy my own company?

Or do I berate myself? Quickly criticize my mistakes? Harp on my failures and ignore my successes? Do I endlessly check social media to find out who is dating who, who bought a house, who is vacationing where, and measure my happiness against theirs?

Dating Boundaries

(CHRISTINA)

Boundaries are required when dating yourself. (Do you trust yourself? Do you like yourself? Do you want to hang out with yourself?) Dating others demands boundaries and is vital to preparing for a healthy marriage.

Being a caregiver by nature, I tended to put others' needs before my own for many years. As a social worker, I listened to people's problems for a living and lost a sense of my own needs in the process. It was a learned behavior that stemmed from my childhood, but something I perfected in adulthood. Compassion fatigue set in.

Your patterns are influenced by your culture and gender. I personally saw my mom give to my sister and me often and endlessly, and I repeated this pattern. I wanted to be a "nice girl" as a kid, receive approval, and grow up to be a good person. Sometimes our self-perceptions cloud our judgment. We give our needs away to people who cannot fulfill them and wake up resenting the very people closest to us.

Giving up your boundaries leads to unconscious martyrdom, resentment, anger, passive aggression, and downright self-sabotage of your own happiness. As women, we are socially conditioned to sublimate our needs for our partners, and this upends even the healthiest partnerships.

We need to give ourselves a nice fence of healthy boundaries, but we also need to be careful we're not plowing down other people's fences and trying to take away their boundaries. If you are fixated on being right or micromanaging your spouse, you are probably infringing on others' boundaries and you are in for a sad story.

A healthy marriage does not keep score—ever.

Marriage is not a game, a match, a competition. You both are always on the same team. If you don't get that rule, it will sabotage your progress and eat you up inside. Keeping track of love, trying to quantify or budget your actions undermines your goals.

Success in marriage is not measured or tallied but felt and experienced every day. It is lived based on how you feel about yourself and your partner. Yes, that changes as your marriage evolves, but your marriage lives in your heart. Healthy boundaries help you value yourself and trust your partner to not keep score.

Then, and only then, are you able to be life-giving and generous in loving your spouse. Yes, it's an oxymoron. I'm selfish enough to be able to selflessly give to my husband. I am radically self-accepting so I can offer my best self to my life partner and best friend.

50/50 Doesn't Exist

(Christina)

One of our friends insisted on dutifully tracking her childcare and household responsibilities with her husband. Who did what when and for how long? If she took her son to school, her husband needed to pick him up. She cooked four meals per week and he would then cook three. Then the following week they'd switch up. Every minute was calculated and had to be made "equal."

She would travel by herself and count the days she was away from home and then her husband would match his days away to hers. The tallying magnified as their son grew, but it began early in their relationship. Chores were calculated and it all had to add up equally.

My friend and her husband divorced. They never wanted God as part of their relationship, they never fully learned to trust each other, and, as a result, it was a relationship that relied on calculation and control instead of trust.

Ultimately, the lesson is clear. Do you trust yourself and your partner enough not to keep score? Are you willing to sacrifice your needs, not knowing if you will ever be reciprocated? Can you let go and surrender your marriage to God?

You Cannot Give What You Do Not Have

(CHRISTINA)

You cannot give what you do not have. You cannot put out what you need if you hold onto it for yourself. You are ready for marriage when you trust yourself in the relationship you've always had—the relationship with YOU.

Do you honestly take care of yourself? Do you uphold your priorities? So much of what I learned is that if I don't put myself first, no one else will. It's my responsibility to nurture myself, to say "No" to others so that I can put my physical and mental health first.

If you value health, you eat well, work out, go to the doctor, take breaks, get good sleep. If you don't do this, what happens? What are the consequences? For me, I cannot think straight or be present when I do not have enough sleep. I must get rest to be at my best for others, and if I compromise this, I limit my ability to contribute to others, which weighs on my happiness.

If you value God, you pray, meditate, seek worship, etc. This doesn't mean you always go to church to worship. This is more about whether or not you find quiet time with God, away from the noise of life and your mind. These are some areas to contemplate.

If you value education, you attend class, complete your homework, seek tutoring if you need help. You find ways to expand your learning by attending college or pursuing a certification. You seek out scholarships or financial aid if you cannot afford it.

How we live our daily lives reflects our level of trust in ourselves, others, and God. Trying to control who does what and when in a relationship will kill joy and love.

When you can't voice a "No" or "That's not right for me," it's extremely difficult to recognize yourself let alone your ideal mate. When you can't get to the root feelings of your mistrust, then you set you and your partner up for a power struggle.

It is emotionally imperative that you trust your partner enough to reciprocate. It's a parallel process. You earn trust and earn credibility with yourself by setting limits, and then you learn to build trust with your spouse.

When Javier and I started dating, we had layers of trust and mistrust to build and break through simultaneously. We were both hurt in past relationships. We were understandably cautious, but we had also done a lot of self-reflection and self-love to be "relationship-ready."

It looks easy from the outside looking in, but a healthy marriage is a constant inside job.

I hear, "You are so lucky! You have a great husband."

We get what we get because of how we have prepared ourselves to receive. This is because I'm a child of God, but it's also because I did the work to look inward, build healthy boundaries, and love myself. And it didn't happen in a day!

One of my biggest lessons learned in regard to boundaries has been about understanding addiction for what it is and what it means to be an enabler of an addict. In many past relationships, I unconsciously contributed to bad behavior and was disrespected. I denied my own needs in order to "save" the other person and came away more broken, depleted, and rejected.

You Don't Need a Partner to Be Whole

(CHRISTINA)

As a young woman, I did not understand how codependency could affect my relationships, especially when it came to maintaining healthy boundaries. I was not aware that my fear of being alone and on and off again depression were not the optimal motivators when choosing partners.

In college, I struggled to wake up and leave an emotionally abusive relationship. I could not hear my friends' warnings. It was like I was brainwashed and it took me two years to break free. Unknowingly, I was running a marathon to bolster my spiritual strength to finally declare, "No more!" and have it really stick. Over time, as I gradually learned to set healthy, clear boundaries, I no longer attracted partners who hurt me.

When I was in my late twenties and first learning these skills, I dug deep into what makes me tick. Why did I let others' needs come before my own? Why did I feel so adamant that I was incomplete because I was single? Why did I put myself down by comparing my life to others, which was unfair, cruel, and often ridiculous? Why did I even entertain so many negative partners who were so broken that they could not heal themselves, let alone encourage me?

Many of my past partners had families with addiction issues. Addiction is a disease and a violation of boundaries— of self and others. Since it is a disease, it cannot be fixed or changed by someone else. I had to let go of my rescue fantasy and recognize I come first.

During my twenties, I would disappear, become invisible, and serve my partner. My boundaries dissolved, and I sacrificed myself for them. This behavioral pattern drove me to go deeper for answers in my life. Only when I turned to God for healing did my suffering bear fruit. I learned that I was worthy of love and that I didn't need to complete myself with a partner.

I am whole, perfect, and complete just as I am. I am a daughter of God.

This spiritual awakening and growth transformed me as I did not have to fill myself with unhealthy relationships. I prayed for a partner but there was no desperation in my soul. I was finally at peace. I remember going on a silent retreat, and after all the struggle of not talking and receiving validation from others, I tuned into the fact that I was a child of God. It was a very simple moment of realization that no person or thing could complete or fill for me. I was one in my relationship with myself and God.

I left an emotionally abusive relationship and moved to California to start a new life. It was bumpy as I relocated and re-invented myself simultaneously. In this vulnerable state, I went back to church. I searched for a spiritual home and found one. I worked in the church bookstore, took classes, and eventually got involved in church leadership. God came back into my life.

I started practicing yoga and joined a gym (and, actually went!) My yoga studio was three blocks from my apartment and I would go almost daily. I lost weight and felt physically strong for the first time in years. I began to meditate, pray, and slowly reclaim myself. I met women and neighbors who were on very different journeys, but I grew in my confidence and my depression and anxiety subsided.

Due to this spiritual renaissance, I began to make better choices about my health, my diet, my friends, and how I spent my time. I realized that I was in charge of my life, not society, not my friends, not my parents. It was a rebirth in that I did not feel the need to compare myself to others. When I actually looked closer, many other people who were my yardsticks for past comparison were struggling, overworked, and unsatisfied.

My faith anchored me. I dated more selectively and turned away from partners who dragged me down or were just looking for a "hook up." I remember distinctly walking away from one date who was literally begging me for a kiss on the lips after just meeting him. I promptly said, "No, thank you!" and left. I had no idea how I was going to get home at the time, but I completely rejected the situation and put myself first.

I grew in my self-respect and set boundaries with my family by not coming home for every holiday and exploring other options. I went on a church retreat at Thanksgiving and attended trips with friends. This felt liberating, healthy, and opened my eyes and my mind.

I began setting boundaries at work by taking on projects only with appropriate timelines and voicing my opinion about professional strategies (which did not always go over well.)

When you shift your power inward and claim your truth, not everyone is there to cheer you on. You are breaking a pattern of behavior and acting "out of the norm." In other words, you might encounter initial resistance from the ones you love or regularly see. They may or may not get used to it, but hold your ground and stay the course. It's worth it for your sanity and peace of mind.

With these internal changes, I built clearer boundaries in my relationships. I came closer to God and started to depend on Him to fill me. It was a gradual and gentle process that validated my worth and my purpose.

The Ah-Ha Moment

(CHRISTINA)

When I met Javier, things were great...until we hit some bumps. After about three months, he started to have emotional outbursts where I became his caretaker. Later, I would feel frustrated and unheard in my own needs. At that point, I became aware that I could easily lose myself in our relationship; I realized I needed to stop falling into my codependent ways and stand on my own two feet, saying what I felt and setting clear expectations.

I did not go to family or friends for advice. Therapy helped greatly. In tough moments, I went to God for comfort and support. I realized that God had to be the center of our dating relationship if we wanted it to work despite our human brokenness.

I learned to establish some basic boundaries within our relationship. Once I saw that Javier could accept those boundaries, we got engaged. We knew our faith had to be the center of our relationship to get us through the challenges of marriage.

Throughout our engagement, I realized that I needed boundaries with my family as well and that only God could be intimately involved with our marriage. This was mostly grace because I do not remember making a conscious decision, but I never wavered in my trust that God would guide us and support our marriage.

My internalization of boundaries took time. I still revisit these struggles in our relationship, and it's a theme that can reappear during times of stress. Fundamentally, I learned that I would never be "filled" by anyone but God. I had to learn to care for myself. I had to learn to stop relying on men and even my family to fill me. With God at the center, I learned to love myself. This opened me up and prepared me for the most wonderful union with Javier.

> *"Love yourself enough to set boundaries. Your time and energy are precious. You get to choose how to use it. You teach people how to treat you by deciding what you will and won't accept."*

> —ANNA TAYLOR

When you trust God to love you, you trust Him to hold your relationship up and get through the discomfort and conflict alongside you. Our humanness cannot save us; we can make the best choices, but life will still come at us, upend our progress, and challenge our security. Lean on your faith and look at your decisions daily, individually, and together as a couple. Pray for yourself, pray for each other, pray for your relationship. Never stop praying.

Our boundaries are our road map to knowing where we begin, end, and overlap in God's eyes. They are our trigger points, our spiritual sensors, our spiritual exit lanes in life which keep us going on the right path or derail our journey completely.

Embrace what you need, what you prefer, what you like. Those feelings are there to guide you and empower you to create a life and relationship that serves you and others.

Take time to reflect on your boundaries.

Learning to Love Myself

(JAVIER)

What is your definition of healthy boundaries? Are they internal or external? Are we being realistic when we set those boundaries or are we accommodating others?

Our childhood wounds and our past do not define who we are as a person. To avoid having our past pain project a false image of ourselves, we can create internal and external boundaries that can support us in our future marriage.

God doesn't want us to feel ashamed, guilty, unworthy, or angry inside. These feelings will bring you down and fuel devastating thoughts and actions. It is like a domino effect, the more negative-based thoughts we experience, the more we are not growing as a child of God but distancing ourselves from him.

The moment that we seek those feelings we find strength, appreciation, recognition, and forgiveness. We become closer to God by creating internal boundaries; our personal growth exponentially increases when we are holding Jesus Christ's hand.

With the loss of my mother, my internal boundaries suffered. I carried the "poor me" attitude and would expect others (especially women) to fill the hole my mother's absence had left. I expected them to be both romantic partners and mother figures to me. My lack of boundaries would sometimes demand that they not set boundaries—that they fill both the mother and girlfriend role. This hurt many relationships. After all, feeling sorry for someone can only carry a relationship for a short time.

Sometimes I would use it to my advantage. By telling someone that I lost my mother at the age of two, I became the center of attention. People were sympathetic and felt sorry for me.

During a *Cursillo* weekend (a men's retreat to bring men closer to Jesus) in an Adoration service to the Virgin Mary, I had a moving experience of understanding the pain that my mother went through when leaving me on this earth. It was a life-changing moment. I saw my childhood through her eyes and empathized with her journey as a mother.

Through that experience and others, I came to understand that I needed boundaries with my childhood wounds. I was done leveraging my sad story to my advantage—to get attention or see myself as a victim. I learned to honor my mother for living through cancer to give me life and recognized how difficult it was for her to leave me behind.

We grow in our faith and spiritual maturity when we re-define our past and forgive and love what happened to us. Our wounds usher in growth and wisdom if embraced.

The loss of my mother created confusion and sorrow. But the deeper truth is that my mother gave me life, which is bigger than all the pain of the past.

As I learned to let go of my past wounds, to rely on Christ as my comfort (rather than women to be my mother), and to be my own hero rather than seeking validation from others, I was ready for the next step: preparing for marriage. This demands your willingness to put your partner before anyone else. This is a new type of boundary and it can be difficult to navigate when we have other people in our lives we care deeply for.

∼

When I was thirteen and my father died, my brother, Miguel, took me in. He became my legal guardian. Miguel was twenty-four; I was thirteen. There is no manual to help you raise your orphaned teenage brother. It was not easy for him. I loved my brother. I was intensely loyal to my brother. And I felt I owed him everything, especially for taking me in.

The problem was that I never felt like my debt was paid. I supported him out of loyalty and loneliness; I had no one without him. I put Miguel first before my own wants or needs, sacrificing what I wanted to do in my mid-twenties to support his dream of having his own business. Every time my brother made a business decision, I passively followed. I was a partner on paper but not in reality.

This lack of boundaries came as a result of a painful childhood that was not fully healed. I still had to learn to trust my own voice—my own needs—and navigate my life. Every decision at that time—my ambitions, my dreams, who I hung out with—was aimed to please my brother. I felt that I had to earn his love again and again and again.

~

When I became engaged to Christina, I freed myself from this pattern. At thirty-four, I finally followed what I wanted in life. I began to express myself more freely and let go of the dating mistakes I made. I started to trust in the future God had for me. I finally let go of decisions that didn't serve me and began to believe that an amazing future was possible.

At times, I would regress and put my brother before everyone else. Since I couldn't always see this tendency, I carried parts of it into my marriage. As I continued to mature and prepare for a life with Christina and our future children, I knew it would have to be different. I had to learn that, even though I still loved my brother, I could separate myself from him.

I began asking myself one basic question: "Who do you want beside you in bed when you are about to say goodbye to this earth? Cleary it was my wife, then fiancé, Christina. My relationship with God helped me trust the process of letting go of the past.

Creating healthy boundaries with my relationship with my brother created a much better relationship in the end. Living with the feeling of being indebted to someone is no way to live. It's not good for either of you.

Remember that you are in control, you are the one creating the relationships in your life.

Use this moment to reflect on who brings you up and who brings you down, always putting your future marriage as the priority.

Reflect on:

1. *When is it hard for you to say "No?" Can you set limits between work and your personal life? Do you put your health front and center?*

2. *Do you surround yourself with people who are supportive and want the best for you? Do you have people in your life who do not support your success and/or your marriage?*

3. *What boundaries do you think you might apply before your marriage date?*

CHAPTER 4

Know Who You Are as an Individual and as a Couple

"Fear not, for I am with you; be not dismayed, for I am your God;

I will strengthen you, I will help you, I will uphold you with my righteous right hand."

—Isaiah 41:10 (ESV)

Becoming Self-Aware

(CHRISTINA)

Self-love leads to self-awareness. When we learn to unconditionally love ourselves, we make better choices. We learn to forgive ourselves more quickly. We treat ourselves with more kindness, patience, and respect.

By turning down the cacophony of self-criticism in our heads, we turn up the volume of God in our lives. We remember to go inward, pray, embrace silence, and cultivate space in our days so that we can find peace, invite discernment, and listen to God.

Knowing oneself is a never-ending process—a lifelong pursuit of seeking wisdom about what you value in your life, how your actions reflect your beliefs. and where and how you spend your time. So often, people say that they want a great relationship, but they do not put in the work or consistency to have a great relationship.

> *"Until you make the unconscious conscious, it will direct your life and you will call it fate."*
>
> —C.G. JUNG

We may say that we value and appreciate our partner but we make them wait while we check our phone, drift off while they are talking, forget to kiss or hug them upon leaving or arriving. If we don't acknowledge our partner fully at the moment, how can we show that we value them?

Actions matter. Every day. Our lives are crazy distracted by text alerts, viral videos, and 24-hour news. There is always a reason to get sidetracked, procrastinate, or avoid a courageous conversation. Over time, these dodgeball moments add up and before you know it, you're roommates if not texting penpals.

What Owns You?

(CHRISTINA)

When examining your vices, bad habits, and false moves, you realize what owns your life. The good news is that when you realize what these things are, you create the ability to make different choices in your relationships.

Even though I experienced many Mr. Wrongs when dating, they each lead me closer to Javier, my very own customized Mr. Right. By clarifying exactly what I did not want in a partner, I got clear on what I wanted. This internalized understanding brought me to attracting and choosing the right person for me. I do not believe this process is accidental.

God has my back and there are no accidents in our journeys. What we do with our life's stumbles are our business and our choice. Do we want to let life experiences inform us and empower our choices? If so, look at them forgivingly and remember:

Every bad night gets you closer to finding your mate for life!

I know that this perspective is not easy. I struggled for years, as it takes courage to be self-reflective and keep pushing forward. It's uncomfortable. And not necessarily encouraged by the hustle and bustle of life—feeling like it's more about survival and "getting through" versus stepping back and seeing how your navigation and choices may not be truly serving you.

Letting go of relationships is undeniably painful. This is what makes dating so challenging. Who do we get to know and how do we assess if someone is good for us in our life? Do we let fate decide or do we actively participate in seeking like-minded friends, communities, and partners?

Off and on in my twenties, I was disappointed with friendships in my life. Living in San Francisco, all my friends were workaholics and always seemed rushed. They were over-booked socially and I did not feel important. I wondered: Was this adulthood?

I felt second best, an obligation on someone else's social calendar. I would nurture resentment and play the martyr, claiming I was the one making all the plans and doing all the work.

I did not feel like a priority because I did not make myself a priority. My need to be liked sabotaged my need to have peace. My fear of being alone with myself owned me, and I could not enjoy other people fully until I created a friendship with myself.

This theme was on repeat in my early adulthood. When I look back now, I see that I was projecting my rejected traits onto others. I was overscheduled, disconnected, and not present—all the traits that I righteously criticized. Water seeks its own level; I attracted what I put out. Realizing this helped me understand what owned me.

Go to Him when you want to find out what owns you. Go to Him when you most want to give up. Our human minds can only figure out so much. Take the burden off, put it on a plate, and serve it up to God. I say, "Here you go, my sweet Father. I know that you've got my back and I have no clue what to do next."

He always comes through.

What Do You Really Want?

(CHRISTINA)

So much of what we frame as important or sacred in our lives is rooted in what we learned as kids—values, beliefs, and traditions our families upheld and nourished.

Whether we enjoy a certain food, believe in voting or volunteering, or go to the doctor frequently for checkups can be influenced by what we learned from childhood and our families. Our past can influence our future choices sometimes without us actually knowing it at the time.

From a young age, I felt successful at school. I enjoyed it, felt liked, and liked most of my teachers. I knew that it was my mission (and responsibility) to go to college.

My father talked endlessly about the importance of choosing a career and mapped out my potential paths with his many suit lapel pens on paper table cloths at several restaurants. My teen angst made me a tough audience, but I love how my dad kicked my butt and tried to get me to get a clue about my career early on.

I learned quickly that in my world academic success equated life success and that education was vital to my happiness. I studied hard, went to the University of Michigan, and later pursued my master's degree at Columbia University in New York City. I ended up with a full bilingual scholarship that paid for my tuition. Now, I'm an educator. This is not random; we act on what we believe.

What you *think* deeply affects how you approach dating, cohabitation, and marriage. Sometimes we internalize inherited beliefs and traditions without blinking and other times we rebel against our family of origin's traditions, trying not to unconsciously repeat our parents' lives.

My family often let conflict simmer, and inevitably, there would be a big blow-up where past transgressions would come exploding out onto the table. We did not often communicate openly or proactively—it was after the fact and became overwhelming because the big talk was making up for lost opportunities. As a kid, I would shut down and freeze. I had no idea how to react as topics often came out of left field, and I felt ambushed.

My family did not speak their mind at the moment, which built up resentment and pent up hostility. I saw anger as bad or to be avoided. In high school and even in college, I acted out by never being home. I avoided conflict, but I also avoided my feelings of hurt, anger, and loneliness.

Determined to forge a new life to prove my independence, anger, and hurt fueled my drive to be my own person and move out of state. It took years to recognize that I was reacting out of unaddressed feelings. It also took years to make peace with the fact that my rebellion was rooted in the past.

I internalized and acted on the value of higher education while I simultaneously sought relationships that modeled poor communication skills. I fell into unconscious patterns of choosing partners who were not my emotional equals and who were codependent. I had to undo this habit to manifest a healthy, communicative relationship.

How Do You Communicate?

(CHRISTINA)

When Javi and I started dating, we held totally different orientations toward conflict. I was a peacemaker and avoider and he had no fear of sharing his emotions—immediately. I felt like I was dodging super-fast verbal bullets and had to figure out a new gear of emotional response, quick-like!

Our cultural differences (my "*Gringa* aloof" versus his "Spanish in your face") and contrasted upbringings presented massive differences in worldviews and communication styles. I was taken aback by his emotional episodes and felt unprepared and defensive. I remember thinking, *You need to chill out.*

Javi's different orientation to life upended me. When we'd disagree, I would sometimes rise to the occasion and speak my mind, but usually, I would shut down. I became paralyzed and felt attacked. I went into mute mode and then, about twenty-four hours later (affectionately named the 24-hour effect), I would unleash a mini-lecture on what ticked me off and why. It was like a thesis, totally perfect and ineffectual. *Sigh*

Here are some lessons we've learned the hard way:

1. We needed to be fully present for each other, especially on dates. Early in our marriage, Javi and I used to frequent a specific restaurant. This was at the height of Javi's international sales career, and his phone was always ringing with calls from different time zones at the worst possible

moment. One particular evening, Javi returned to our table after taking his phone call. He said that he realized he had abused our time together, turned his phone off, and gave it to me for the rest of the meal.

2. We needed to sometimes abandon being "right" for the relationship. I measured love through words, not actions—saying something cruel in an argument was not fair game. But in Javi's world, everything was on the table, in love and war. And once we made up, it was immediately gone for him. I, on the other hand, remembered it all and was determined to hold him accountable.

    We had to deprogram our predetermined argument settings. It took a lot of love and prayer to get to active listening, with no name-calling or interrupting. We had to turn down the volume on impulsivity, reactivity, and "cray cray" to be able to come out the other side with mutual respect, patience, and patience. No, that is not a typo!

Sometimes you have to sacrifice being right for the relationship. You need to abandon fighting words for a more compassionate mindset. Setting up your marriage for success means letting go of winning or losing an argument. You accept the issue at hand and seek a solution no matter how much humility and heartache it takes.

3. Being spontaneous and showing small gestures of kindness built closeness and gratitude. During our courtship, Javi left little gifts around my apartment and I treasured his thoughtful surprises. One day, I was coming home from work and there he was, waiting at my apartment building's

front stairs with a huge pot of yellow flowers—my favorite kind and color. He was considerate, thoughtful, and romantic. He got the details of love.

It's also okay to show your love in very different ways from one another. This can bring out your authentic love for one another. It may be rough at first to accept your partner's different style, but once you see their strengths, appreciation and trust grows.

For example, I am not romantic. I have never been very sentimental. Who saves love notes? Not me! Yet, I am super affectionate, adoring, and attentive. I would listen to Javi for hours and wake him up with kisses.

I verbally express love. I told Javier how much I appreciated and adored him and I complimented him often. That didn't cut it for him, though. Javi needed "Action, Jackson!" He measured love by behaviors, by acts of service: making him a meal, taking him home after shoulder surgery, and tutoring his nephew to name a few examples. We had different beliefs and behaviors in demonstrating love.

Like pretty much everyone, I gave what I craved—verbal recognition, praise, compliments. "Proof" was words spoken and written. Javier desired affection, attention, and action, acts that showed self-sacrifice to prove my love for him. This difference could have divided us very quickly. Our trust in our love and one another was tested many times and would break down from time to time, and we would then build it back up.

Yet, our differences did not have to divide us. We learned more about what each other needed to feel loved and then we each acted on it. What saved us was creating an environment that brought us back to our romance. It was light-hearted, forgiving, and real. Even when engaged, we savored every date and moment alone together to hold each other's hands, walk in silence, and just be.

We all experience challenges in expressing our love. Collect and cultivate those simple together moments. Sprinkle in some romance kindling to keep that fire going. Those memories will hold up when the mundane crazy of life tears you down. Your differences are part of your chemistry and what can actually drive you closer.

Stress Magnifies Our Differences

(CHRISTINA)

Differences in our individual beliefs imploded before our wedding day. I was disappointed with one of my family member's lack of emotional support throughout our engagement and marriage preparation. Concerned that I was upset, Javier rallied for a confrontation immediately. In fact, he strongly believed that I was too passive and I had to confront this person's actions and deal with this behavior before the wedding.

He felt that I was choosing my family over him, as I did not follow his advice. It became a crisis of trust that I could not wrap my head around. Looking back, we were both facing the biggest commitment of our lives and fears were heightened.

We talked it out and prayed and talked it out some more. We attended a marriage preparation retreat, which later became our ministry and ultimately our life's work. Javier's fear of abandonment kicked in and my need to please and keep the peace made me buckle down.

My reaction was to retreat, deny, and let it all go. I did not have the energy or stamina to address the situation head-on.

The dysfunction was "normal" to me and I wanted to "get through it" and "not rock the boat."

This difference of opinion brought up our significant cultural differences as well as contrasting communication styles. Growing up, Javier and his family had big blowouts—people passionately stating their mind at the moment and even walking out of situations (homes, restaurants) on the spot. Bam! The upset eventually blew over, but no one feared or even stalled confrontation. In fact, they welcomed it. This was a different reality for me.

In my family, we let our feelings stew and simmer. My learned approach was to let things remain dormant, holding onto them and building resentment for years. Sometimes, family members would unleash years of anger when provoked during a crisis.

Anger, hurt, disappointment usually remained underground and family relationships suffered or people became estranged in the process. My parents lost touch with their family members and age-old arguments lingered, killing relationships over time. Leading up to our wedding, the stage was set for both these sets of behavior to collide.

Navigating conflict—how and when to handle it—is a constant challenge or pothole that we still hit in our marriage today. God was putting up a challenge for a good reason. Our contrasts in communication style slowly presented us with work to help us find and cultivate our own way of communicating, resolving upset, and taking responsibility for our behavior.

In the end, this family member sought forgiveness at our wedding. It was an unspoken blessing. Not much was discussed, but the situation was resolved by God's grace. I prayed for no drama, and I got reconciliation. It was quite beautiful.

Call the Shots Together

(CHRISTINA)

This is a harsh lesson that I learned the hard way in many previous relationships when trying to sacrifice my needs for theirs.

Javier will always be passionate and hot-headed. I will always be strong-willed and a peacemaker. How we express ourselves can be a complete contrast at times. We can lock in conflict or carve out our own unique way of being together. This is a lifelong work of a relationship—to make your values, beliefs, and traditions your own as a couple so that they are not inherited or unconsciously adopted, but rather a choice.

When Javier and I couldn't agree about how to deal with my relative, we chose to go to God, seek spiritual counsel, and pray before our wedding. This saved us from catastrophe. Yes, there was conflict and drama, but we were both in it together, not against each other.

Solidifying what you want and value as a couple and acting from that is a lifelong process. We continually reconcile and seek common ground regardless of our stark differences which reignite again and again.

Sidenote: We love our partner's "crazy" when we are dating and in courtship. Their differences and passions are exciting, exotic, and awesome. But those elements that are mysterious and novel wear off fast and can quickly get old in marriage.

The things I loved about Javier also became my biggest obstacles when we were in crisis.

The differences that make you sizzle can polarize you and become roadblocks. Entering a spiritual marriage is about consciously choosing how you want your relationship to be. It can emulate your favorite, most beloved aspects of your upbringing and it can totally redefine unconditional love and how you experience it.

The two of you have complete freedom and the responsibility to one another to actively participate and create a marriage that serves you and makes you grow. Embrace your inner boss and call the shots together.

∾

Gender roles are another key belief area to examine before marriage. We can revert to old habits or let our unconscious expectations affect our relationships in time. For example, how do your gender roles differ in your marriage? Do you expect the woman to do more housework and give up her career to raise your children? Do you expect the man to earn more money and/or be the breadwinner? Do you do all the cooking, do you share cleaning, etc.?

Would you be willing to move to advance your spouse's career? Would you consider both of you taking significant maternity and paternity leave to take care of a new baby? If these issues are not discussed ahead of time, you leave yourselves open to unconscious and unhealthy expectations that will lead you to conflict and/or resentment.

Before Javier and I were dating and engaged, I was pursuing my own consulting business and Javier had a full-time job. He was extremely supportive of me forging ahead. He continued to open doors for me, surprise me with homemade dinners, and we were both eager to start a family. This was a good balance for us of traditional and progressive.

We had "ideas" about how getting married would look, but we really had no idea how it would manifest in your lives. The dream can be very different than the reality so talk about some of your expectations before you get married. Javi and I both wanted to have careers and work even after having children.

Living together can be smooth sailing as you get to know one another while mostly doing fun activities and building the best friendship. There are not the same pressures of "reality" as in managing a joint household, family and work pressures over time, and filing a joint tax return. Transitioning out of the honeymoon period may lead to stark disappointment with the daily grind of household chores, bills, commutes, and financial stress.

We initially wanted three children (this did not happen) and we agreed to be willing to move for the spouse's career (this might happen soon!). These conversations and many more built a solid foundation of accountability and communication for the years to come.

You may not touch on these areas for a very long time, but it is extremely wise and helpful to examine your unspoken expectations heading into the biggest commitment of your life instead of being forced (backed into a corner) by unexpected circumstances.

Our Past Does Not Define Us

(CHRISTINA)

I used to be extremely ashamed of my past relationships. Friends and family viewed my past partners as poor choices, dogs, losers, you name it. Since I chose to become involved with these individuals, I took my family's and friends' judgment not as an affirmation that I deserved better, but rather that I had done something wrong and was to blame.

I internalized past relationship failures as my secret shame, burden, and personal defect. In fact, I felt extremely unworthy of a healthy, supportive partner because my track record wasn't so hot—there must have been something wrong with me to attract these people into my life.

I condemned myself, and I wouldn't let up. My self-talk was negative, and I would cry and cry and cry at church. I would literally walk in, sit down, and start crying.

I would torture myself—comparing myself to my younger sister who married her high school sweetheart and never dated anyone else. Who can measure up to that classic love story?

The thing is, it was a self-fulfilling prophecy—the more I inwardly hated myself for my past mistakes, the more I sentenced myself to misery, becoming imprisoned by my loneliness. All of this filtered my reality.

At one point, I remember going online (when Match.com had just started). I met a lot of inappropriate men who were looking for one-night stands and equating dinner with rights to my body. They were most often emotionally stunted, poor conversationalists, and immature. Clearly, God was showing me: Wrong way. Go back!

It was a bummer of all bummers. Yet, again, my heart sank. What was I doing wrong?

I could not figure out why God was leading me through this darkness. At many points, I would get down on my knees and beg, *Can you please show me the way, Lord? How can I find my perfect match?* Bargaining, begging, pleading, I was still in the wilderness.

It was only when I was so broken and desperate that I began to look to Him fully and surrender the outcome that I heard His words in my dreams: "Let go, I got this. Your husband will come to you. Stop looking."

This was a clear sign. I needed to stop all the frenzied dating and sit still, look within, and love myself. Instead of looking outward, I needed to go inward and become my own best friend and confidant.

> *"It is in the broken places you are*
> *most often used by God."*
> —Christine Caine

I took up yoga, went on spiritual retreats, became involved at church. I built a fervent prayer practice and focused on all the blessings in my life. Instead of fixating on what I did not have, I gave thanks for all the many beautiful people and experiences in my daily life.

I arrived at this new mindset kicking and screaming, but a change was happening. A new day had come and the past was no longer part of me. I put faith first, before myself. What happened before in my life no longer held me hostage. It could not touch me, and I was free to experience what God had in store for the future.

After many years of introspection and pain, I began to appreciate the tough times. My loneliness led me to a deeper faith in God, which became an endless blessing in my marriage and in my life. I would not be the person I am today if I did not trudge through the wilderness.

I would not be in the marriage I am today if I did not go through those turbulent times. It's like Winston Churchill's quote, "When you are going through hell, keep going." Remember: we don't know what we don't know. Our path is all part of God's plan, and it takes days, months, and years sometimes to believe this. But it is the truth.

We are healing whether we realize it or not.

If you have not found your perfect partner, do not despair. Remember that your past is not your future. You are a perfect child of God and all mistakes turn into wisdom if you allow it. Do not compromise your integrity to be loved. Hold out for respect and remember you are worth the very best. God wants this for you!

On our first date, Javier held the door for me and I hesitated. He looked me in the eye and said, "I never want you to open the door for yourself. I want to always do this for you." It was real; he meant it and I deserved it. This was not just an act of chivalry but of deep regard and respect for me.

I absorbed that respect in every piece of my being. God showed me that our past does not define us. It does not limit us and it certainly does not scare us. It can set us free because we become different people from it and share our wisdom and lessons with others. Our greatest suffering is our biggest gift and blessing.

Speaking Different Love Languages

(JAVIER)

When folks ask me about my in-laws, the image of the movie *My Big Fat Greek Wedding* always pops into my mind. Christina and I are complementary opposites. We are Yin and Yang. We are opposite to each other in many ways, but we support each other.

It has taken time to come to this place in our relationship, however. At first, I was a bit rigid in my personal values. Growing up, I felt that if a person didn't think as I did, there was something wrong with them.

My father used to say that you can tell someone that you love them, but that doesn't mean anything. Words can be carried by the wind. What matters are the actions that you do for that person. I took this to heart and always showed my love through actions: romantic dinners, gifts, and acts of service.

$\sim$

When I was courting Christina, I was always on the lookout for proof to pop up— reassuring me that she loved me. Christina, on the other hand, valued things that were written or verbal such as love notes, but that didn't do it for me. Christina would tell me that I looked handsome or that she was proud of me, but it didn't sink in. My response in my head was, "I'm just ordinary." Actions are what matter to me. I wanted her to put me on a pedestal in every situation that we were in. Even though we both shared physical affection, I struggled to know that she appreciated me.

I waited for more actions, but all I got were beautiful notes and tons of compliments and the words, "I love you." That created friction in the beginning and some doubt. Once again, my childhood wounds were popping up, creating a reality that was not actually there. I felt that those beautifully written words were not from the heart. I created excuses as to why I couldn't accept the love Christina was showing. I didn't realize at the time that trusting people to love me was hard for me to digest.

As time passed in our marriage, I wanted to design the best relationship ever. I decided to journal three positive observations about Christina every morning for one whole year. In the beginning, it was more natural. Over time, I needed to dig deeper to find her strengths. This ritual transformed how I saw my wife.

I began to see the beauty of how she was trying to communicate, and it was easier for me to embrace her differences. I learned not to change her values but to add them to our combined strength in our marriage. I learned to communicate more thoughtfully and calmly. With time, I was able to own my point of view without having to see it as the "right" way of thinking.

We all have gifts, talents, and strengths. It is so easy to look at your future spouse and think of his or her weaknesses and flaws. But that won't get you where you want to be.

When you combine your gifts, talents, and strengths as a couple, a beautiful, collaborative outcome is created. We are concentrating on what brings forth the best of us. You and your future spouse will feel empowered to work together. Jesus Christ didn't walk the earth telling us about our weaknesses, but he was a constant reminder of our strength if we followed and gave our hearts to him.

Our Faith Is Our Own—
Not Our Family's

(Javier)

My faith is something that I carry very deep in me. Finding and understanding it, however, took several years. My father was raised Catholic, but he raised me as an atheist. The only thing that I inherited after his death was a book in Spanish titled, "How to be an Atheist." I never read it, but it is sitting on my bookshelf as a reminder of how far I have come.

Even before I fully understood my faith, I always wanted to be married in a church. I believe that marriage is not just a binding contract or an agreement, but a spiritual vow. It is a promise and union that you make to each other for better or worse. For me, it is a sacrifice of selfish desires when we commit to looking out for the interests of our spouse and family.

I was baptized as a baby, but since my father was an atheist, I never received my First Communion or Confirmation. It took thirty-four years to receive those Sacraments.

I always knew that there was a higher power; I felt it in my heart. But the day I turned my heart to Jesus was the day my dad passed away.

It was shocking when I heard the news, and at first, I didn't want to believe it. I was called out of my classroom at school. When I got to the office, my brother was there and I could tell he'd been crying. They informed me that my dad had passed away from complications from his recent surgery.

I was in shock. I tried to convince myself that my dad went on a long trip and he was going to come back. But he didn't. Eventually, I broke down in tears. And then I cried my eyes out every night for years.

The third night after my father's death, I remember very vividly being in my oldest brother's house. I went to bed in the spare bedroom. I could hear my siblings discussing the funeral arrangements. I missed my dad so much that I started to cry and felt very lonely.

I kept asking, *Who was going to take care of me? Who was going to be there while I was growing up? Who was going to tuck me in at night?* I felt so lonely and desperate for an answer. Suddenly, I felt and heard a powerful and calm voice say, "I am, my son."

From then on, I knew that my Heavenly Father was with me all along, loving me as I am His child and protecting me throughout the year. Because of Him, I am alive. I am not six feet under, in jail or living with a substance addiction.

When I met Christina, I didn't want to come across as a "Jesus Freak" and a recruiter from the church, but I knew at some point I'd need to let her know about my faith. She was attending a non-denominational church in San Francisco. I was attending a Catholic church in San Jose, where Father Jim inspired and challenged me to be a better person every day. On a wall outside of the church, it says, "NEVER GIVE UP!"

As Christina and I got to know each other, I was surprised to learn that Christina was raised Catholic. That led me to introduce her to Father Jim. She loved my church, and we decided that even though we came from different cultural backgrounds, we wanted to build our family in the Catholic Church and raise our children in the Catholic faith.

Knowing myself has been the greatest challenge in my life. I inherited many beliefs and values from my family such as loyalty, hard work, standing up for myself, and respect for women. These were good things. However, I knew I didn't want them to be the only things. I knew I wanted a life with faith at its center.

In order to accomplish this, I had to alter some of the beliefs I'd learned as a child. I had to adapt and grow in the direction I felt was right. Once I married Christina, I reprioritized my beliefs and values even more to match our union. This included individuating from my family and letting go of the need for their approval.

Parts of this road have been rough, made harder by my childhood abandonment issues. My marriage and my faith working together have helped fill that void and heal my heart.

Knowing yourself is a lifelong journey. But it's one worth taking.

Letting Go of Baggage Makes Room for Joy

(JAVIER)

We all carry baggage throughout our lives. Some carry a backpack, some drag oversized luggage, and others push an overflowing shopping cart. We treasure each piece of baggage even though they bind us to shame, sorrow, embarrassment, depression, and negative self-talk.

Our past is part of us, but it doesn't need to bind us like a tether or a noose. The energy of holding onto the past takes such a toll on us that there is no room for anything more. Being afraid of letting go is so deep that we carry it throughout our lives.

I carried a mountain of baggage for many years. Each piece had a different origin. This included growing up in a dysfunctional family, the death of my mother, experiencing abandonment at an orphanage, the death of my father, and coming to the United States alone and afraid at thirteen. I collected feelings of unworthiness, shame, embarrassment, and guilt and held onto them.

I entered my marriage with two full shopping carts. I didn't want to let go. They were my burden and my comfort. The more I dug into them, the worse I felt. My baggage provided me with a sense of security. The negative self-talk even convinced me that I could not let go of them and the past. I was born this way and I simply had to accept my circumstances and live with it.

The problem with entering into your romantic life with two full shopping carts of luggage is that they are a reminder of what is to come in your future relationship. Let me explain. Those shopping carts are living in your house, your yard, your car, your bedroom. They go everywhere with you. They are in the way of your relationship between your future spouse and you.

As you grow in life and in your relationship, you create new experiences and meaningful moments together. You need room for the new. Where will this go if you are pushing your loaded shopping cart everywhere? There is no more room for joy.

I rejected the new experiences at the beginning of my marriage. I loved being near those shopping carts full of luggage, but they got in the way of my growth with my wife and the new life we wanted to create together.

My baggage was a barrier to my relationship with Jesus; I knew I needed to let it go. The only way for a plant to grow is to put it in new soil. Asking for forgiveness from God and forgiving myself opened up space in my life to kick those shopping carts to the curb for good. I won't deny that I always keep a backpack…just in case (we all do). I soon realized how extraordinary my marriage was and how close I got to my Lord, Jesus Christ.

The Struggles of My Childhood Gave Me Skills I Could Use in Marriage

(JAVIER)

The loss of my parents is the most significant pain in my life. Their loss was the catalyst for everything that happened to me. The loss of my mother brought abandonment and deep loneliness throughout my childhood.

I felt that there was something wrong with me and that's why my mother was no longer with me. I felt inferior because when friends came to my house, I couldn't introduce her or have her watch over us as moms do. I was always embarrassed because it was just my dad and me at the school activities.

The loss of my father was devastating; it broke me in half. I have never felt so lonely or lost in my life. I don't wish the loss of a loved one on anyone. It changes you forever.

When my oldest brother told me that my dad passed away, I lost my breath. I could not breathe due to sharp pain in my heart. After his death, I added more baggage to the shopping cart. I developed trust and anger issues and armored my heart with a coat of sarcasm. I was even voted as the most sarcastic person in high school.

When I look back and examine those incidents, I see how God used them to equip me with strength. The loss of both my mother and father made me more independent than any other child my age during that time. I was paying rent, cooking, cleaning, and working at a job.

Not having a motherly love throughout my life helped me understand what a gift mothers provide to their children. I have an immense appreciation for the opposite sex and how so many amazing women make this world a better place.

The loss of my parents let me appreciate how strong, resilient, and smart I became. It provided me a warrior mentality that I developed and cultivated throughout all the obstacles. I never gave up and continued moving forward no matter how bad things got. I learned to look at life and see the beauty in others and really appreciate the simple things in life—because when it is gone, it is gone.

Your past might be dark, gray, or sunny. But no matter how dark, gray, or happy dandy it might be, there are always strengths that you can dig up to make you appreciate how you pulled through.

Letting go of the burden of past pain opens you up to a new relationship with your partner. This is essential; you need all the new space you can find. Letting go of what brings you down will bring you up and others up around you, too.

I had to readjust some of my childhood beliefs. Self-awareness is key to strengthen your relationship with your future spouse—accepting the values and beliefs that are ingrained in you and respecting hers can enhance your life.

Reflect on:

1. *Have you forgiven yourself for mistakes in past relationships? Have you sought healing from God? Do you accept that you are not defined by your past behaviors and past relationships?*

2. *Have you seen the blessings in past painful experiences? If not, look at them differently or pray for a new vision that empowers you, heals you, and makes you even stronger.*

3. *What choices do you make consciously or unconsciously in your life? How do your relationships mirror your own traits and behaviors?*

4. *When you feel frustrated, are you able to invite God into your life to show you how you may make different choices?*

5. *How will you spend the holidays? If your families do not live locally, do you split them up? Will you trade family visits from year to year?*

6. *How do you want your marriage to emulate and/ or be different from your family of origin?*

7. *What beliefs about marriage do you have that might undermine your relationship success?*

CHAPTER 5

Getting Right with God

*"But he said to me, 'My grace is sufficient
for you, for my power is made perfect in
weakness.' Therefore, I will boast all the more
gladly about my weaknesses, so that Christ's
power may rest on me. That is why, for Christ's
sake, I delight in weaknesses, in insults, in
hardships, in persecutions, in difficulties.
For when I am weak, then I am strong."*

—2 Corinthians: 9-10 (ESV)

My Faith Journey

(CHRISTINA)

Both my parents were raised in the Catholic church and both
of my grandmothers were ardent, devoted believers their entire
lives. They were spiritual warriors, and I hope to emulate their

faith and commitment. Being Romanian, my mom experienced church in the Byzantine Catholic tradition. Mass was in Romanian. My dad didn't understand most of their wedding ceremony. My father attended Catholic schools his entire life, including a Jesuit high school. He was briefly in the seminary but left as a teenager. The oldest of six kids, he worked to help pay for his private school tuition (as did his siblings).

My sister and I were both baptized in the Catholic tradition and attended Catechism (faith formation classes) until I was in fourth grade. I do not remember much other than I had a Catechist teacher say that she could talk in "tongues" and it scared me. My parents pulled my sister and me out of the classes and that was the end of attending "Catechism." Our family slowly edged away from going to Mass, and by the time I was in high school, we did not do church at all.

As an elementary-aged child, I remember talking to God frequently in prayer before bed and throughout my day. I remember thanking Him and sometimes bargaining with Him. Volunteering in an after school program ignited my passion for social justice, and God was leading me even though I was not cultivating a relationship with him.

Looking back, I wish that I had sought God in my life earlier. I took a long and windy road. Working after college in New York City, I would visit Catholic churches, but nothing clicked. I didn't feel at home or called to return. I guess you could say that those were my lost years.

I was longing for God but did not name or fully recognize it. I was in graduate school for social work, and I found deep fulfillment in my work. I now see that this as a starting point for my ministry work in social justice. But I did not know God in my daily life.

Are You There, God?

(CHRISTINA)

It was only when I moved to the Bay Area that I really prioritized my spiritual growth and sparked my relationship with God. I attended many churches and landed in a nondenominational church in San Francisco. There I truly experienced going to church in a tight-knit, loving community, one that had my back and lifted me up. I felt supported, accepted, and loved unconditionally. It was like coming home.

I took many classes in metaphysics and meditation and attended many retreats. There was a lot of seeking. I was open to learning and experiencing any form of enlightenment possible and discovered the power of prayer. It was like I experienced a reunion with a long-lost part of myself.

The night that I met Javi I had just come from a yoga retreat, and I was at peace. I felt calm with myself and my spiritual relationship with God. It was a beautiful window of trust. I recognized that I was not in control, and I didn't want to be. I hit a sweet spot of surrender.

I gradually internalized my self-worth by turning to God. This meant that dating was off the table. I prayed with close friends to let go of the past and welcome God into my life. I surrendered my desire for a partner to God, trusting his timing and eternal wisdom. Here I turned a corner in my spiritual maturity. Looking back, I don't know how I got through my teens and twenties without Him.

Once I hit thirty, I recognized that I was not a victim and my relationship with God was not a rescue fantasy. He was not a hero to my damsel in distress. I had to talk to God, listen to God, and look to God's guidance in my life.

It was a three-dimensional relationship that did not include bargaining or begging for a certain outcome. I was His child, but that didn't mean I acted like a child. I had to let it go and give my desires to Him. I had to get out of my own way.

I had to come to that moment on my knees, giving up in order to receive more. It's a spiritual paradox that was lost on me for many years. When Javier walked into my life, I did not need him. I did not feel that he was there to complete me or even validate me. I felt that he was there to share my life and create a spiritual journey together with God and as a couple. I was open to love him, but I definitely embraced and loved myself. I was not able to change for someone else and was not expecting him to change himself either.

So much of my relationship with God has healed my relationship with myself. I see now that He was always there, waiting in the wings, trying to guide me on the right path, and often protecting me from danger and destructive decisions throughout my life. I had Him in my heart, but I did not look to Him first or even second. I was confused and it was not until I released negative experiences with my past Catechism teacher to create a vibrant and active relationship with God.

∽

"The strongest marriages are built on a foundation of shared faith. The more you love God, them more capacity you will have to truly love each other."

—DAVE WILLIS

I have no doubt that it was God's plan that Javier and I met. We were set up on a blind dinner date that took a long time to arrange. I knew Sheila for years through work and we became friends as well as colleagues. She was married to Luis, who was Javier's first friend when he came to the United States in middle school. We had talked about introducing the two of us but the timing was off for a while, and finally, when it was right, they set it up right away.

Living in San Francisco, I was driving a Honda Civic and had a peace sign sticker on my bumper. Luis told Javi that I practiced yoga and once Javier saw my car, he was convinced that I was a hippie vegan. His heart sank.

Fortunately, I was the first person to dive into the main dish and stab my fork into a piece of beef. Javi's fears diminished and he felt relieved. I laugh at this example because our human minds are always making up stories about other people when God knows best.

I was reserved; he was charismatic. He was sarcastic; I didn't miss a beat. He "interviewed" me about having any past relationship luggage, and I reversed the questions, which he happily answered.

He said, "You know. I don't trust *'gringas.'*" I placed it right back in his lap. I retorted, "That is your issue. Not mine. Work on it."

There are advantages to dating in your thirties—you know what to ask and are brave enough to be honest. There was no messing around. We did not have the time or energy to play games.

We kept it real and it was refreshing. The more faith you have in God, the less likely you fear to show your true self. It was a feeling of liberation. And, no matter the outcome, I felt free to be myself.

We ended up hitting it off, giggling like teenagers late into the night. Upon saying goodbye for the evening, he said that he would call me the next night. He did and was right on time. From there, we started a new life together.

When you let go of control, you surrender to God's plan and open up to more possibilities. There are no coincidences and every single event happens for a reason, even those we cannot see or understand. Through trusting in God's divine plan and design, we are led in the direction that gives us the most peaceful ride. Healing my relationship with God turned the tables so that I could not take to heart the failings of my life. I could release the past, focus on the present, and know that in the future, "the best was yet to come."

Let God Be Your Rock

(Christina)

When Javier and I started dating, we wanted to attend a church together. My relationship with my San Francisco church was shifting, as the pastor recently left and my church family grew apart. It was a rough transition, but it presented an opening for something new. Javi suggested that we attend his childhood Catholic church, as the priest was dynamic, radical, and extremely open.

Even though it was a big change, I was curious and immediately liked the priest's humor and honesty, as well as the accessible, humble setting. It felt safe, which was exactly what I needed.

I returned to my childhood rituals of Catholicism. The comfort of knowing the sequence of Mass brought up feelings of familiarity and a sense of security. It was like a spiritual homecoming to get married in the Catholic church. The priest was a hero of Javier's teen years; I was sharing that part of his life with him.

We soon learned that if we wanted to be married in the church, we had to attend a pre-marriage retreat called Catholic Engaged Encounter. Our priest did not present it as optional and we were all in. Upon arriving, we felt instantly at ease by the facilitating couples' warmth and humor. One of the couples was bicultural like us and we could see ourselves getting more involved.

At the time, we had no idea what a huge impact Catholic Engaged Encounter would make on our lives or how much of a foundation it would become for our own marriage. Immediately after the retreat, we volunteered to help out by welcoming couples at future retreats, and we began to form relationships with the community. During our engagement, we attended another weekend retreat to observe the leaders while simultaneously writing our talks to then present at future retreats.

Stepping up to serve God and others changed our lives. We dug deep to share our own fears and insecurities. We moved the dial on our feelings of inadequacy. By exposing hard-learned lessons from past family struggles, our commitment grew.

Catholic Engaged Encounter held a pivotal role in strengthening our marriage. We learned from older couples in our communities, saw inspiring role models for healthy marriages, and gave back by supporting other engaged couples. While revisiting our own courtship and feelings of love for one another, our marriage reignited and the mundane struggles of daily life subsided. We were able to see the big picture of why we were together and what kind of life we wanted to create.

Attending an Engaged Encounter wedding preparation retreat changed the trajectory of our marriage. We did not know it at the time, but taking time away from our home, daily lives, and technology set us up to tackle bigger questions about our values and dreams before saying "I do." This was vital because so many topics were lingering on the surface and we needed the space, time, and encouragement to go deeper.

The bicultural differences in our families felt pronounced and heavy. We learned to accept our family members for who they are and to forgive them and ourselves. We began to acknowledge that our differences in our upbringing and experiences affected our expectations—about everything.

We talked about how to celebrate holidays and whether we would adopt if we could not have children. Our comfort level grew in discussing sex and intimacy, sharing finances, and how to tackle debt. We discussed how we felt about things such as vacationing separately, going out socially with friends of the opposite sex, or making large purchases without our partner's knowledge. The list went on.

These conversations were set in a tone of holding God at the center. By upholding the goodness of the person and putting the marriage first, we became more open, creative and introspective. We were not drafting up a laundry list of "I want . . ." or "Give me . . ." It was a generous, vulnerable conversation about how we expected our lives to grow and open to one another. It was about how we needed to utilize our faith as our key go-to strategy in life versus our own problem-solving skills and/or the demands of others.

When you put faith at the center of your marriage, you actively seek spiritual and personal growth as your compass.

This is counter-cultural and can be scary. When you view marriage as a sacred act, as a pact with God, you start to recognize that you are your own family and forging a new paradigm. If you and your partner step into marriage with faith at the core, it can usher in massive personal growth and a possible upheaval of unconscious patterns that have stunted you in the past.

God works in His own time, but going to Him before getting married can certainly bless your commitment and show you where there is work to be done.

That said, it's a long haul. No doubt. Javi and I have had crises of faith and felt estranged or forgotten in our marriage and by God. But He's there every step. We veered off the path, and when we showed the smallest inkling of interest, He stepped up and worked miracles in our lives.

Put your faith first or certainly keep it at the center of how you approach your relationship and marriage. By letting go of your own fears, you will expand your consciousness to embrace a divine grace that will bless you for many years to come.

When you do good and speak good, good is yours.

Nothing is lost on God.

Analog vs. High-Definition

(JAVIER)

Growing up, my Dad told me that you only have one friend in life, the rest are just acquaintances. I no longer believe that to be true, but I have learned that there is one special relationship we must focus on. A relationship exists before we are born into this world. It is the relationship that we have with our Holy Father. He is just waiting for us to remember when we come to this world.

Even though my Dad was an atheist, I always grew up believing that there was a higher power. I wasn't formally raised Catholic since I never attended faith formation classes in the Church, which my Dad detested.

However, in Madrid, we lived five hundred yards from a church. Every time I entered my home, I saw all the activities that happened there.

Later in life, after my brother took me to Mass and my journey began with Father Jim, I thought, "This is it! This is my church." I attended regular services, donated money, and crossed my arms for a blessing instead of receiving communion.

I never thought of getting involved in a ministry or attending a class for my faith formation. I was going through the motions. At home, I would do what I had always done. I prayed to "get stuff," to bargain but not much more.

I was attracted to spirituality without really knowing the importance of it. It was all for me, what I could gain and acquire. Church made me feel good. Father Jim's services were enjoyable. My life kept going along, and I prayed without feeling God's presence.

My connection at the time was what I called analog. There was a connection, but not a 24/7 relationship with him. There were many times in my marriage I wished that I had a "high-definition" relationship with God. I know He was listening and trying to show me all the things happening in my life.

But I wasn't ready. My relationship with Him was self-centered. I was a child at heart. My attitude was, I am doing what I need to do. *I am attending church, giving money, and getting a blessing.* What else was there? Perhaps I could pay more attention during the homily?

It was during my *Cursillo* (a spiritual men's retreat) experience, that I realized the love that God has for us. I was curious and excited. I heard so many good things from friends that I was curious to experience the weekend. My spiritual network line upgraded to high-definition. I understood Christianity was not all about routine and worship, but about action.

Christianity in action became my new purpose. How can I mimic Jesus Christ and give back to my neighbor the same love Christ was giving me? I understood that truth more than ever. I changed from the inside out. The more I embraced piety, prayer, and action, the more my relationship with God grew like wildfire.

As I felt this truth in my bones, I saw my relationship with God as a blessing. I transformed from victim to victor. There is no day that I do not ask myself, "What does God think of this situation?" or "How can I leave my self-centered relationship and give to others with unconditional love?"

God Is Your Primary Relationship

(JAVIER)

You might ask, "What about your relationship with God has to do with the pre-marriage stages of my life. What does God have to do with all this?" Everything! The more you enhance your relationship with Him, the more you can feel the love that He has for you.

God will make the most beautiful moments in your courtship even more radiant. And He will transform the darkest moments into times hope and support. He will shine that light wherever you go and pick you up when you fall.

As we all enter the preparation for marriage, there are always peaks and valleys. There is the great excitement of courtship, meeting the parents of the bride and/or groom, and planning the wedding day.

Our childhood wounds, values, beliefs, and family-of-origin themes will all show up with intensity. If you have the Boss on your side, things will run much smoother. You trust the process; you know that something greater is at work. God gives you freedom, peace, and love.

It's Not About the Wedding

(JAVIER)

We fell in love with our pre-marriage retreat—San Jose Engaged Encounter. During that weekend, we prepared for our journey into marriage having no idea how much we would be given. Christina and I were thirsty for a faith-based family. God was first in our journey, but we had no idea where to start.

Our intention was simple. We gave our engagement and marriage to God. He knew best. When I proposed to Christina, we began designing our life together, mapping out goals for years 5, 10, 15, 20, 25, and on. Before we started the vision process, we knew that we needed a foundation on which to craft our marriage.

Be wary of making your wedding the focus of your engagement. It's tempting to autopilot through the bliss of the event. Expand your plans to how you want to feel after the ceremony. Your intentions will grow in a magical way. Autopilot doesn't change the speed or direction. Make sure that your wedding is not the focal point and that you are truly establishing a union with God first and foremost.

As we planned out our lives together, it took a lot of trust. We had to be open to the long-term desires of the other person. It isn't easy for me to trust, and it was hard for me to do this at times.

Before we married, I placed all the cards on the table. I decided to be as honest as possible in everything that was happening inside or outside of me. I had to be completely myself to open up to the love Christina had for me.

Trust is precious to me; I don't give it away easily. Growing up, trusting others was very difficult for me. The indirect abandonment by my father and my siblings created mistrust in anyone that wanted to get close to me.

Becoming aware of my childhood wounds, I realized that I needed to trust the person I was going to spend the rest of my life with. I needed to fully lay down all the cards on the table, to be vulnerable and trust my future wife—the one who was going to hold my hand before I say goodbye to this world.

At first, this was hard because I assumed that Christina would judge me. When I let in her unconditional love for me, I released all my fears. To this day, I am completely myself with Christina.

I had a traumatic childhood, and now, I express my true self without hesitation. It is so liberating! I love being as silly as a child and Christina's best friend in life. I can show all the parts of myself and be loved.

Planning past the wedding will be so much more rewarding than simply focusing on the big day. It will open you up to the joy, and sometimes stress, of focusing on long-term dreams. It will force you to be open and trusting with your partner, and it will reward you with a deep connection that you'll be able to foster through your life together.

Prayer Is Our Therapy

(Javier)

Our faith grew when we prayed together more as a couple. Prayer is essential if you want to have a relationship with God. As you pray as a couple, you become vulnerable and honest with your future spouse.

You might do a prayer of Thanksgiving to God for bringing your spouse into your life. You can offer up your gratitude for all the joy and fulfillment you experience together. You can ask for guidance, support, hope, and faith that the hardships will be guided by God.

Praying together builds intimacy in your relationship together. Christina and I can get into super deep conversations and analyze problems up and down. We can make up plans, flow charts, mind maps, but nothing except prayer gives us the peace of mind we need.

Let the Holy Spirit into your struggles as a couple before your wedding and during your marriage. Choose your faith in God during your courtship as your guiding principle to help you make decisions together.

Creating that habit of prayer is more than a lifesaver throughout your marriage. It is inviting the best advisor, father, therapist, and power into your lives to make them whole and healed. It is celebrating every moment and acknowledging your source and why you are together.

Reflect on:

1. *What is your relationship like with God? How do you build your faith? Do you trust Him to bring you the best despite feelings of disappointment or hurt in the past?*

2. *How might you nurture your faith to bring you more comfort and peace in your relationships? How might you let go of the past to open up more possibilities in your current or future relationship?*

3. *Do you feel comfortable praying alone? Together?*

4. *Pray as a couple. Start with what you are thankful for in your relationship and what you would like to create in your future together. Perhaps you can offer something up for God.*

5. *Pray for your perfect partner if you are single. Know that he or she is out there. God will orchestrate the perfect meeting. Be grateful that He always has your utmost happiness in mind.*

CHAPTER 6

Courtship

*"So they are no longer two but one
flesh. What therefore God has joined
together, let not man separate."*

—Matthew 19:6 (ESV)

Ending the Dating Game

(CHRISTINA)

Both Javi and I experienced a whole lot of "unhealthy" before
we found one another. Looking back, we find it humorous,
but I don't want to minimize the experience—it was downright painful and ugly at many points. Javi half-jokes that he
would never remarry if I died mainly because dating is so very
challenging. The upside of dating is that it can be viewed as a
period of discovery.

In healthy relationships, people don't play games; they act like their true selves from the beginning. Intentions in dating can be difficult to discern. In our secular world, it is acceptable to use dating as a fast track to a "hook-up culture," avoiding commitment, let alone getting to know oneself. Both Javi and I noted that so much of our dating experiences were ripe with self-posturing—looking good—to be accepted and attractive because we did not fully accept and love ourselves. The outer world mirrors the inner world and that can be disturbing, especially if you are not clear on what you want and what you stand for.

In healthy relationships, you're comfortable with who you are and don't let dating change that. Many times I would say, "Why am I attracting people who are deceptive or unkind?" In retrospect, I feel it was because I was not honest with myself. I felt so much pressure to be coupled during my late twenties and early thirties. So much of me being "successful" in life was defined by being in a relationship, heading toward marriage, and on the way to starting a family.

In healthy relationships, you don't compare yourself to other couples. You follow your unique path. I put suffocating pressure on myself, comparing my journey to my younger, already-married sister and coupled friends. I was stuck in comparison, and it led to unnecessary stress and suffering.

> *"Far too many people are looking for the right person instead of trying to be the right person."*

—GLORIA STEINEM

Due to this self-criticism, I could not be myself with others. Parts of me rebelled against this marriage pressure, and in doing that, I did not embrace my own needs. This led to me dating men where I ended up as the caretaker, substitute mom, and enabler.

Ultimately, I arrived at the conclusion that being myself was not only enough, but the only solvent way to approach dating and creating a healthy relationship. It may have taken me a while to arrive at this conclusion, but it radically changed my world. Not only did I fully accept my own values, needs, and preferences, but I also cherished them and embraced my desire for a match that saw me for my true self. I then was able to see dating as an opportunity versus a burden; an adventure instead of a task.

Learning to Let Go and Let God

(CHRISTINA)

Therapy helped me identify where I was hurting so I could acknowledge that the past no longer had power over my present. Prayer, attending church, and developing a spiritual support network at church and with like-minded friends bolstered my self-image and what I deserved in a partner. I will never forget my friend Sheila saying to me, "You never want to be dating someone who makes you cry." That may seem like a no brainer to you but it was revolutionary to me. I tolerated so much pain and discomfort that I had forgotten and betrayed myself in the process.

When I saw how God loved me unconditionally, I learned that I deserved better and I began to forgive myself. I let go of my past mistakes and did not make dating about me. In fact, I detached from the outcome of having to find a husband and took the pressure off. What happened is that my desire for dating diminished. Instead, my focus became seeking friendships that supported me being my best self, which meant cultivating a deeper trust in God.

The burden was miraculously lifted. I did not have to do anything or force anything to be loved. I did not have to achieve a successful relationship or put more effort into the dating process to make sure "it all went right." What I got, which radically changed my life, was that I actually didn't need to do anything. I was in the arms of God and all I had to do was trust the process—his will for me—and to be open to what came next.

It was humbling, and sometimes disturbing to my over-achieving, perfectionistic self. So I was just supposed to sit back and let "Mr. Right" come to me? Wasn't that a bit passive or even lame? Didn't I have to earn my right to a relationship and actively seek my perfect match? Of course, we need to make some effort, but I was exerting all the wrong kinds of action. I was trying to control the process to quiet my fear of being alone, incomplete, and unworthy of love. I was trying to build the boat and row it while directing the current of the sea. This is not possible. I was exhausted and burned out. Finally, I just said, "Stop, self." I rested to reset, get quiet, pray, and let God take the wheel.

Rock Bottom Can be a Great Starting Place

(Christina)

Sometimes we need to fail in order to learn. From dating the wrong person, we learn what we do not want in a partner. That is valuable information that can make relationships look different for all of us.

Sometimes the twenty-story nosedive from a skyscraper or the cosmic two-by-four wakes us up to our unconscious patterns and creates more in our hearts. We become aware of our limited human consciousness.

Even though I felt alone in my single years, I had to learn to trust God's will in my life. By not finding Mr. Right, I got very clear on who he was. After being cheated on repeatedly, criticized privately and in public, stood up on dates, ignored, and even slapped in the face, I recognized what constituted emotional and physical abuse in relationships. Most importantly, I finally saw that I did not deserve this treatment.

By falling into a pattern of dating abusive men who took no responsibility for their actions, I recognized that the common denominator was me. This realization did not excuse their behavior, but it liberated me to make different choices. I was not responsible for their behavior. They were. Period.

Once I began to forgive myself, I turned to God. He taught me to love myself and that taking care of myself was my new mission. I felt empowered instead of victimized. I don't want you to have to go through what I went through, but no matter what you go through, I know that if you turn to God, He'll help you through it.

It was a long road to get to this place of acceptance, but all the pain brought me a deeper understanding of who I am and His love for me. Failure and heartbreak can yield amazing results in that you risk, you lose, and you learn immensely about yourself.

This is a spiritual oxymoron— you give up control to get it, and that is how life works.

God's Plan Is Always the Best Plan

(CHRISTINA)

When I found peace with my single status and cultivated joy in my life, Javier walked into my life. It wasn't a coincidence or good timing; it was God. I felt grateful for my work, my family, my friendships, my home—all the blessings that I could not embrace earlier.

My mindset focused on celebrating life now versus fixating on what is missing from my life. Instead of giving all my power to solving "my problem of being single," I embraced my freedom.

I asked God to lead me where I could serve; I delved into the possibilities of life. I traveled, visited friends, and practiced yoga. I went on meditation retreats and nurtured my interests. It was a renaissance of self-acceptance.

When you teach yourself how to be treated by being your own best friend, miracles happen. With God as your unconditional companion, you expand your capacity to love a partner. You no longer worry, stress, or freak out about how it is going to happen or if it will happen. You focus on the present, the beauty of the moment, and remember that everything is in divine order. It will come to you when you are ready, when he is ready, and when the environment is at its best to support your relationship.

Javier often says that he wishes that we met earlier in life—high school, college, or earlier in adulthood. But we both know that God's plan is always the best plan. We met when it was perfect for us. We spiritually marry each other again on our anniversary because we are always growing, changing, and recommitting to ourselves, God, and one another.

We were not the same people that we had been before we met. In order to come together at the perfect time, our lives had to have many experiences so we could converge at the optimal moment.

Learn to trust the process and trust God.

Remember that no matter how long you know your partner, you are always learning about them. Each moment is new even if you have a long history or a sordid past. We must recognize the past's lessons and embrace the present so we may hold onto our faith to create the most beautiful union.

Honesty with Myself and My Partner

(CHRISTINA)

So much of my life before Javi was shrouded in feelings of ambivalence and fear about dating and relationships. Due to painful relationships in the past, I was hesitant and doubtful that I could find an equal who loved, respected, and cherished me for who I was.

Moving to New York City after college and then recreating my life in the Bay Area were both bold moves, exciting choices that enriched me, but also brought unique and lasting challenges. Both times I had to rebuild my support network, adjust to a new job, city, and community, as well as face feelings of loneliness, displacement, and inadequacy. My risk-taking came at a cost, and I healed through it, but it certainly brought challenges and sadness.

I had a push-pull relationship with my family, and I sought my independence away from them, but I also needed their emotional support. I struggled to find that balance, and in some ways (in retrospect), I made it harder for myself. It was my unique path and I hold it dear to me now. Depression does run in my family, and until I accepted myself, bouts of sadness and all, it was hard to come to terms with my feelings. I rejected them, denied these periods of paralysis, and tried to cover them up by working harder or packing my social calendar.

Truly, aside from therapy, my relationship with God has transformed my feelings about depression. Not only did the frequency and intensity of these dark periods of sadness shift, but I found an entirely new level of support and trust in my life's purpose.

I understand that depression is complicated and unique and I still continue to seek treatment, but having God as part of my plan has definitely helped.

The freedom of being honest with myself about what I truly wanted in life paved the way to greater intimacy with God. I could confide in Him my desire for a husband and a family. I owned my deepest desire with no shame. Instead of rationalizing why I could not attain what I wanted or entertaining fears of the unknown, I reframed my experience as a vital, necessary journey that God created for me and my optimal development. Being honest about what we want in our lives is a key ingredient in attracting it and manifesting and maintaining it for years to come.

Javi made it easy for me to unveil my unbridled self. He showed up fully in our relationship with his preferences, needs, and fears squarely on the table. He did not waver or water down who he was or what he desired. His willingness to be real, vulnerable, and fully himself was a gift from God. It was permission and an invitation for me to not apologize for any part of my past, present, or future and put down my guard.

During our first meeting (a.k.a. the interview), Javi asked if I had past luggage from ex-boyfriends. I thought this was hilarious. We all think it, but who says it when you first meet someone? I said, "No." but he pressed for specifics.

He continued, "Do you have any of your ex-boyfriends' phone numbers in your phone right now?"

I laughed, "No." I did not have their numbers as I did not believe in keeping in touch with ex-boyfriends. I understand it's a personal choice, but I needed them out of my life.

∽

When you give yourself permission to be honest about who you are, what you believe, and what you want to create in your life, you are relationship-ready. You don't make up excuses, lie to yourself or your partner, fall into the "disease to please" by saying what you think others want to hear. You hold firmly onto yourself and dive into the conversation fully present, no airs and no shame. "Hey there! This is me. This is what I stand for. This is what I believe." Many people do not recognize this early or before getting involved with a partner, and their expectations, hopes, and needs are hidden, repressed or even denied by themselves.

Javi was never intimidated by my strong political beliefs or career ambitions. He never rejected my opinion as less than his and certainly did not diminish my thoughts or needs. The more I showed up as myself, the more I felt accepted and loved. This was clearly reciprocated by me for Javier, and we grew more and more connected.

When you do not have to apologize for who you are, you are free to give relentlessly because there is no attachment to the outcome. You offer yourself freely and remember your true nature—you are a child of God. You do not have to prove that you are lovable.

In order to be spiritually ready for marriage, I made peace with my past, loved myself—shortcomings and all—and held true to my beliefs and desires like they were worth it every step of the way. Essentially, I learned to not give up on me, to not play small, and to not surrender myself to someone because I did not believe that I was worthy of being loved unconditionally. By accepting myself, I harnessed total honesty with Javier. I did not hold back my likes, dislikes, values, perceptions, and needs. I showed up as my true self and did not apologize or hide behind a mask. It was blissful to be seen, heard, and appreciated for who I was.

The Language of Respect

(JAVIER)

I wonder how men understood women before we had books, traditional media, magazines, radio, TV, and social media. Let's imagine many years ago, books were kept by the monks, prophets, rabbis, and scholars. Social norms mostly came from one's family and town.

If your family was in the faith, you would most likely learn from those Christian values, your community and culture on how to date a lady. In *The Godfather Part 2*, I love watching Al Pacino's character start to date in Sicily. He is followed by half of the bride's family via chaperones throughout his date. I love this—the idea that her entire family is watching over her, that they know she deserves the best. Women deserve this level of respect.

Today, we are inundated with images of unhealthy behaviors in relationships. Online pornography, over the top talk shows, and televised dating contests depict women as sexual objects for men's pleasure. They often have to fight one another by using their sensuality and are degraded in the process.

When I learned about "sexting," (people sending explicit sexual photos and messages via phone) my jaw dropped. Many of the teens in my youth ministry said that this is how some boys get girls to be interested in them. The boys peer-pressured the girls to send them explicit pictures via text. Then the girls would feel pressured to have sexual relationships to avoid being shunned socially—in person or online. The boys felt pressured to assert their sexual prowess via photographic proof of their conquests. It was hard for me to comprehend on many levels.

Pornography often portrays women as objects. Many men participate and/or are educated by violent and degrading messages about sexuality. For many people, viewing online pornography is becoming a normal behavior. Many people are deeply confused about the intimacy and emotional implications of sex and how it relates to their self-worth. By viewing these images, they forget the love that God has for them.

My father influenced me, and I treated women with respect and reverence because of this. Every time I saw my dad interacting with a woman, I was mesmerized by the way he was so respectful to them. He used to tell me, "Son, always be a gentleman because we are a dying breed." This included always opening the door and never walking ahead of a lady when walking with her. Many women I dated would call me "old school." However, it was what I knew fit my beliefs and values. I loved opening the door for ladies, escorting them to the car, and looking for small details to make them feel important. Being a romantic was ingrained in me, thanks to my father.

"The way you win over a lady is by making her laugh." This second piece of advice from my father became my mantra and I applied it to my dating life.

Just before my father died, his visits to the hospital became more frequent. He knew that he was going to pass away soon; he was very sick. He accelerated his mentorship with me to prepare me for courtship and marriage. He emphasized that I should always be myself and never tell a woman that I loved her if I didn't. He encouraged me to not focus on a woman's outer appearance. Every lady shines and has different beauty on the inside as well as on the outside.

Let Your Faith Be Your Compass in Dating

(JAVIER)

Our faith empowers a healthy dating life. We are all broken inside, but God's hope frees us from the past and heals our wounds. Like attracts like, so as you embrace yourself fully, not only do you release baggage, but you also attract people who are growing and healing like you.

When I met Christina, I committed to love myself more than ever before. But, it was a long road before that moment. Before I met her, I spent five years of my life living in a relationship that shut me down. I was miserable and it had slowly caused me to believe that I deserved nothing more.

I told myself that if I was homeless, that would be a better choice than living a life of misery. Somewhere deep inside, I knew that God was telling me this—that it wasn't his plan for me to be so unhappy. I was compelled to trust God and put my worries and fears in the back seat.

Finally, I decided to end this rocky relationship and move out. I had no idea where I was going to live or how I was going to support myself due to my horrible credit and having a declining business with my brother. I put it in God's hands. I knew that if I made a conscious decision to love myself first, God would lead me in the right direction.

That day, I gave my adorable Doberman pinscher, Luna, up for adoption. My sister suggested I check out a rental apartment complex. I was hesitant knowing that I had horrible credit and had no idea how the next month's rent would be covered. I placed my faith in God—that everything would be okay.

In less than two-and-a-half hours, I had keys to a tiny one-bedroom apartment. There was no furniture and no food, but it was mine. Six months later, I met Christina. I had a great job and my apartment was fully IKEA-furnished.

It was all God's plan. Surrendering to Him and accepting to love myself brought me closer to my dream and meeting my wife, Christina.

Be an Open Book

(JAVIER)

When I see two people flirting with each other, I immediately think of the dance that birds do when they are trying to mate. The male puffs himself up and expands his wings to attract the female. He makes himself bigger than he really is.

As humans, we do the same thing. We inflate our ego—especially us males—to the point that many online profiles are full of lies. In person, we do the same. We make up things about ourselves, pretending we are someone we are not just to get that attention.

If the relationship grows, we will run out of ways to talk about ourselves. This will backfire as you hurt the other person. It's best to make sure that we take the mask off before we do the courtship dance.

I have always been an open book—with nothing to hide. I share everything with everyone, even strangers. My wife sometimes tells me to keep it to myself, but I honestly don't care. I don't care about being judged because your opinion is none of my business. There is only one person who can judge, and that is God.

The first day I met Christina, I shared my whole story with her. I told her what was important to me, from my family to watching Real Madrid. I told her about my past, including my most recent relationship. I told her I realized in that relationship I had not been showing myself love, and I did not want to settle. I remember clearly how I set the tone. I said, "I'm not looking for fast food but rather a home-cooked meal." I wasn't interested in dating and seeing where the wind would blow. I was looking for the person who was going to be there with me until death.

Knowing what you want out of the relationship is part of being honest with yourself. I learned the hard way that I was doing more harm to myself by settling instead of looking deeper into myself. I had to learn to ask myself what I valued in life, how I wanted this relationship to be, and how my gifts, values, and talents would play into that. Sometimes we marry a cat, hoping we can turn them into a horse. This isn't good for anyone. We either need to accept our partners how they are or free them.

The best way to do this is to look inside ourselves and ask, "Do I value the dreams that I have or am I going to settle because of status, image, or because I want a 'trophy spouse'?"

When I met Christina, I told her all about my relationships, the bad and good. I told her of my failings and my successes and where I was going in life. I told her what I dreaded and what I wanted out of my life with someone. It might seem brave to take that approach, but I had no fear that I was going to lose her. In my heart, I knew that we were meant to be. I felt peace knowing that I was starting a relationship with a clean slate. I knew that I was committed to having the best relationship ever.

Reflect on:

1. *Am I truly happy in my current relationship? Am I free in my relationship to express my needs, likes, dislikes, and what I believe?*

2. *Do you treat your partner as you want to be treated? Do you both feel respected and cherished?*

3. *Can you let your guard down and express your fears, hopes, and vulnerabilities with your partner?*

4. *Are you willing to love yourself unconditionally right here and now?*

5. *What parts of yourself do you hide or deny in relationships? How can you bring them to light so you can further your honesty, and thus intimacy, with your partner?*

6. *Do you need to disclose something to your partner? Communicating BEFORE marriage can not only prevent years of mistrust, shame, or disappointment but unleash a deeper sense of safety and acceptance. Find the time and say what you need to say.*

CHAPTER 7

Commitment

*"Therefore a man shall leave his father
and mother and hold fast to his wife,
and the two shall become one flesh."*

—Ephesians 5:31 (ESV)

Becoming One

(CHRISTINA)

The balance between self-love and love for others is a lifelong study. How do we nourish ourselves, our faith in God, and also be the best for our partner? So much of what I internalized (even though I did not realize it at the time) was to give up myself for my partner. I sacrificed my needs because I thought that was the right thing to do, when in actuality, I ended up forgetting who I was.

Similar to maintaining healthy boundaries, giving the best of ourselves does not mean that we must suffer, feel ignored, and then slowly grow resentful. The practice of being "life-giving" is about leveraging your love to go above and beyond your ego to empower and support your partner in a loving way that may feel inconvenient at the time. We don't have to be crushed under our "relationship," but sometimes we will need to make sacrifices for our spouse, and those sacrifices benefit us in the long run. This comes with recognizing the difference between being right and being kind. When you invest in your partner's well-being, even when it's not the easy road, blessings come back to you twofold.

Generosity doesn't have to be a grand gesture (though it could be). When Javi and I were dating, we worked crazy hours building our careers. We did not make it a priority to cook meals at home. I vividly remember coming home one night from a long workday to find the table decorated, the house lit with tea candles, and a home-cooked meal ready to eat. Javi had rushed from a soccer game forty-five minutes away to make this happen. It was a gesture that set the stage for our relationship and marriage. Sometimes we do things that are inconvenient or difficult just because they benefit our spouses.

And it doesn't have to be sweeping in scope. It can be simple kindness like preparing a cup of coffee or tea and delivering it to your partner. It can be a small gesture like an encouraging text or a handwritten love note. You can make a meal, clean up afterward, or do the other person's laundry. These examples may seem mundane, but in daily life, they go a long way. For me, when Javi meets me at work for lunch, I feel special and acknowledged. It's a way to break away from routine and spend some extra time together.

One life-giving act that deeply bonded Javi and me when we were courting was that I offered to tutor his eight-year-old nephew who was struggling with reading in school. I would meet him weekly and take him to the library to work on his homework. I had my own consulting business and the flexibility; why not offer a hand? This really demonstrated my commitment to Javier and his family. That was not my intention at the time—I was just doing what came naturally to me.

Let your love come through your actions. Being life-giving is going the extra mile when you might have to move your needs aside temporarily. However, these acts of service in relationships build trust and intimacy. Think of them as wise investments—they give more than they take in the long run.

In our wedding preparations, Javier was extremely supportive in that he pretty much gave me carte blanche in planning, but also provided feedback when I needed his take. He was insistent that he wanted me to feel like a queen, and though I didn't view the event as such, he made every attempt to have me feel special throughout our engagement. The magic of putting your spouse as a central person in your life is not only special but is contagious to those around you.

Our excitement to get married with God as our guide propelled us to volunteer for Engaged Encounter before we were actually married. By recognizing that your marriage serves as an example of God's unity, you see that it is much bigger than you. It's us and not me. You can leverage your marriage to serve others and positively impact their lives.

Of course, this is a big change and can even bring sadness. You do need to mourn a past way of life—marriage is not the same as being single, but the rewards of unconditional intimacy outweigh that discomfort and loss.

When I say that Javier is my best friend, it's no exaggeration. We cultivated a friendship from the beginning. We have always shared our deepest fears and wildest hopes. We earned one another's trust, which enabled our faith to grow. As we grew spiritually, so did our willingness to put ourselves second and our marriage and relationship with God first.

Marriage is not for the weak. Nothing worthwhile comes easy, but putting God at the center certainly makes it easier. Trust your faith to propel you to do extraordinary acts of kindness for your partner. When you get that intuitive hit to go beyond your comfort zone and offer yourself, go with it.

Don't stifle or repress your generosity. By acting on your love, you build a solid foundation for reverence and compassion. It will fill your cup so when times get tough, you can lean into those memories. This will help you remember the value of what you have and the precious gift of your relationship.

Am I Ready for This?

(CHRISTINA)

Marriage is the most serious commitment in your life and can certainly be the most rewarding. In our society, marriage is often depicted negatively as a power struggle with an only 50 percent chance of succeeding (avoiding divorce is not exactly a high bar). It's wrought with stereotypes of a passive, disconnected, or domineering husband and a nagging, disconnected, self-centered wife. Often it's portrayed as bland and sexless.

Marriage is also falsely imagined as perfect, glossy, idealized—a post on Pinterest. It's portrayed by picture-perfect family Christmas cards (we do this!) and beautiful vacation shots on Instagram (we do this, too!). It's extremely challenging to find the spiritual core and truth about marriage when looking to the outer world. In fact, most people see marriage as a choice, but not necessary and certainly not based on faith first.

Discernment is a spiritual process where you go inward to prayer and meditation with God to ask for guidance in your life, including your primary relationships and major life decisions. You pray alone and together and ask for insight around what you want in your life and what is best for you.

This is spiritual armor against a world that is feeding us negative messages about ourselves and others. Our days are driven by competing distractions (social media, 24-hour news, texting as a substitute for face-to-face conversation) and our true values get lost in the haze. We are all human and vulnerable to these distractions, but you can use your marriage to keep you afloat from the drowning noise. It can be a reminder of the truth, of what matters most in your life, and what you want to create together.

Javier and I knew that our marriage would be bigger than us. We believed from the get-go that two souls unified under God are much more powerful than one. When you put your faith in your relationship before you get married, you find a higher sense of purpose, one that transcends sexual chemistry, attraction, common educational backgrounds, favorite sports teams, and a shared sense of humor.

All in

(Javier)

I used to have a habit that when I started a project, I would be super excited about it. My energy was contagious, and I would rally people in with, "Well, let's see what happens." A good friend of mine pointed out my pattern, and I reflected on his observation. It was like heading out on a road trip and letting go of the steering wheel halfway through.

I soon realized that my hands-off attitude was actually self-sabotage. Most likely, my car would crash or go off the road into a ditch. For sure, I would not arrive at the final destination.

When I met Christina with all my wounds, insecurity, and love for her, I became aware that the Javier who was doing great stuff in his life needed to reflect on what it meant to be married to such an extraordinary woman.

It wasn't about me anymore; it was more about her. I was willing to leave my ego at the door and move into a relationship. It was the best investment that I could make, and it forever changed me, helping create a new life.

The Son of God came to this Earth to give His life. He gave love wanting nothing in return. He came to make us aware that when we are life-giving to another person, full joy awaits us. On many occasions in my marriage, I chose to be life-giving. (Many times I did not.) When I did, my opportunities seemed to flourish and blessings arrived out of the blue.

On our wedding day, I wanted Christina to have her special moment. I was getting married as well, but it wasn't about me. I didn't need the spotlight or people's praise or celebration. All I wanted was for Christina to have her day of perfection. I wanted a fairy tale day coming true.

I decided to forgive my older sister whom I hadn't spoken to for over five years. We invited her to the wedding. By letting go of regrets and frustration of past family incidents, I looked to our wedding day as an opportunity for forgiveness. Out of my love for Christina, I wanted to sacrifice any need for attention or recognition. I wanted to create harmony and bliss for my stellar wife, even if it was awkward or inconvenient for me.

In my heart, mind, and soul, it was all for her. I deeply desired for her to have the best day of her life. I paid attention to every detail, and I engaged her in meaningful conversation. It was like her birthday on a very grand scale. Celebrating her because of who she is. That was the commitment that I made.

It can be easy to please others or go along because you want something in return. Being life-giving is more than mimicking Jesus. He spread His love, kindness, and compassion for us out of sacrifice. By thinking of ourselves as the center of the universe, we go deeper into insecurities. By giving ourselves to our partner, we find peace.

Give Your Love Away

(JAVIER)

During the last thirteen years, we have had the honor of serving over 1,000 couples through our marriage preparation ministry. It may seem socially "easier" or more "expected" for women to express thanks to their partners, but when couples both share gratitude for one another in front of the group, you see their love reflected in the smallest acts. When someone makes even a tiny sacrifice to be life-giving to their partner, it returns tenfold. We all grow when we give without hoping to get anything in return.

Early in our marriage, I helped Christina start her own consulting business. All I saw was success for her. I believed that she would be successful, and I saw her thriving, making a difference with her clients. I jumped in to help with cooking, cleaning, and doing laundry. It was a great ride just witnessing her growth.

Little did I know that all my support would come back to me tenfold when I quit my full-time job to open my own business over a decade later. Christina has been a huge fan of my adventures and rose to the challenge as our family breadwinner. It was a role reversal for our family and our marriage. Her life-giving actions happened without a hitch. There is no limit to what you can accomplish as a couple when you put your love first in your lives.

"When you say, 'Yes" to others, make sure you are not saying 'No' to yourself."

—PAULO COELHO

Being flexible and open to change comes from cultivating a generous heart. Leaving your ego behind humbles you and builds trust with your spouse. I have come to realize that I don't have to be the "macho man" of the house or the king of the jungle. My manhood is not defined by my paycheck. Having a life-giving marriage goes beyond gender roles; it is looking out for the best of your spouse and supporting her in every way.

By releasing our insecurities and control issues, we create an opportunity for growth and an awesome relationship with faith at the center. We receive so much going beyond our comfort zone to give more. The secret is not to wait for the reward; don't be stingy. Pray, discern, and give. Watch the miracles come back. God always provides.

When There Is Smoke, Go into the Fire

(JAVIER)

Marriage seems like a hit or miss proposition to many people, kind of like entering a building and locating every blinking exit sign in case of emergency.

We need to learn to resist creating backdoors in our marriage and take the necessary steps to enter more deeply into our commitment instead of running away from it.

On 9/11/01 when the twin towers were collapsing, there was smoke, fire, and explosions everywhere. People raced out of the buildings, jumped from windows, trampled other people to survive. It was total chaos—people running away from danger at every turn.

Yet, there were a number of other people—God bless them—volunteers, the Coast Guard, private security, police, fire, even random citizens who immediately ran toward the disaster inside the buildings. They ran into the crisis, not away from it. This is what we should do in our marriages.

You probably know that married life is not always rainbows and sunshine. It has its ups and downs, as does everything in life. The question is: are you willing to run into the smoke to *put out the fire?* Are you willing to face issues as they come up and speak honestly about how you feel and what you want?

This is not comfortable or easy. We think of marriage as spiritual hazing. You need to ask yourself: are you ready to commit regardless of the circumstances? Once you are in, go all in. No excuses, no side entrances, no back exits. There is no decision to make from then on—because you will do what it takes—no matter if the fire is burning all around you.

God has our back. We know this because we live it every day. Christina and I went through a very dark time in our marriage, only to come out the other side and say, "God, we are committed to this marriage. Make us right. Heal us as only you can."

Let Go and Let God

(JAVIER)

By surrendering to God in your marriage, you are making the wisest decision. Because you know that your human mind cannot think itself out of everything. And a part of you knows deep down that true love requires true surrender.

People ask how I knew that Christina was the one for me. I share with them that when I saw Christina, I saw us growing old together. To me, Christina is the last person that I want holding my hand before I meet my heavenly Father. I want to look into her beautiful blue eyes and tell her that we had an amazing life together—how much we have accomplished together, how we supported each other in our dreams, how we dealt with the ups and downs of marriage, and how we made the best of the times that we spent together.

When I met her, I didn't want to change anything. I loved her strengths and I loved her weaknesses. She was perfect!

If you don't see yourself growing with your fiancé throughout life, it is going to be a hard journey forward. We cannot change anyone, including our spouse. If we look at each other's strengths, we can cultivate personal and spiritual growth that will enhance the relationship.

If we devote our marriage to God, He will fight the battles for us. He will take the worry, doubt, and fear away. Those emotions lead to destructive behaviors and a negative outlook. It's easier to look for one another's flaws and faults than to find the good and focus on improving ourselves. God helps us let go of our insecurities and create more freedom to love in our relationship.

By acknowledging the gifts that God has provided us, we can be amazed. With this gratitude, relationships can go to another level. We are often surprised by how God has changed our mindsets and our attitude about one another.

Reflect on:

1. What are small things (putting in a load of laundry, visiting your partner at lunch, cleaning up the kitchen) you can do that may be inconvenient but show your love to your partner?

2. How do you feel when you give to your partner?

3. Acknowledge and thank your partner for something (preferably) small that meant the world to you recently.

4. Are you ready to transition from courtship to engagement to marriage?

5. Are you personally ready to make that commitment? Are you ready to pull the trigger in making it happen?

6. Do you need time to reflect on what matters most to you?

7. Discern. Pray to God and pray together. Take time before entering the lifelong commitment of marriage to know in your bones that this is the right decision and right time for both of you.

CHAPTER 8

Sex and Intimacy Before Marriage

*"Therefore a man shall leave his father
and his mother and hold fast to his wife,
and they shall become one flesh."*

—Genesis 2:24 (ESV)

Intimacy Is More Than Sex

(Christina)

There can be much confusion and pressure regarding what constitutes a healthy sex life in dating. "Hook up culture" normalizes one-night stands and objectifies bodies as disposable vehicles of self-serving pleasure.

Online pornography is a massively high-profit industry and is often a child's first exposure to sexual activity. Society's distorted views on sex and sexuality thwart and hinder healthy expectations about sexual and emotional intimacy and often create destructive power dynamics where individuals are demeaned and disrespected.

Infidelity and lack of commitment is the number one reason why marriages end in divorce. This often starts in dating. It is increasingly challenging to decipher our own sexuality in a social framework that doesn't respect our values or our partners. How do we negotiate our sexual needs and fears? How do we ask for what we want sexually? How do we talk about sex and our limitations before marriage with our partner? How can we create sexual intimacy that lasts in our relationship and also includes a deepening of trust and reverence for one another?

Expressing love through caring for your partner's needs builds intimacy. This involves a continuum of verbal, non-verbal, and physical cues and acts that deepen over time. For example, love and sexuality are intertwined in how they are expressed in marriage. Being generous to your partner's preferences and also concerned about their emotional safety during sex is the foundation of nourishing trust and lasting intimacy in an ongoing sexual relationship.

Sex is not the same as intimacy, but it certainly can be an expression of it. Many times, we take for granted our attraction to our partner and spouse. Even in long courtships and engagements, we can overlook what initially attracted us to our mate. It is extremely important to actively rekindle your attraction and admiration for your partner and revisit the novelty and initial romance of your relationship. This may be super easy when you are engaged and excitedly planning a wedding, but after the honeymoon, "reality" can set in and you may become disenchanted.

The key ingredient to a healthy sex life is embracing the full continuum of sexual intimacy in your relationship. Love is expressed in many ways and we tend to give what we like to receive. It's like when you're shopping for a birthday gift for a good friend and you can end up buying something that you would really like. This is a natural human tendency.

> *"The goal of sex is the big O... (and it*
> *ain't orgasm). It's Oneness. Loving the*
> *whole person, not just the body parts.*
> *Connecting at a deeper level."*
> —Tim Gardner

Whether you choose to be sexually active during dating or not, you want to be talking about sex from the get-go with your partner. Go to God and discern what is right for you. If you both decide to choose abstinence before marriage, it is important to have an open and clear conversation about this expectation as well. It is helpful to continually check in with each other as it can be challenging and feelings may shift throughout the relationship.

It is tempting to rush into sex, especially when you are dating, because there can be a strong physical attraction. It is so important, however, to make sure that your sexual relationship is rooted in your emotional relationship and that you both feel safe to share your feelings and fears. This builds intimacy, trust, and ultimately creates a much deeper connection.

Leveraging Your Love Languages

(Christina)

There are three main ways in which we demonstrate our love for our partner: verbal, physical touch, and action:

- Giving verbal compliments such as a direct "I love you," offering praise, and saying "thank you" are all verbal demonstrations of love.
- Physical acts include touch (hugs, handholding, a squeeze, a peck on the cheek) and build intimacy and closeness for others.
- Finally, behaviors and actions can demonstrate love: making dinner for your spouse, picking him/her from work, helping with a work project, etc. We all have different ways of showing our love and wanting to receive it.

For Javier and I, we express our love differently. I am a verbal person, so I wanted and needed cards, love notes, and "I love you's" as proof of our love. You want what you give, right? Javier preferred acts of service, so follow-through on a promise was key for him. If I said I was going to do something and did it, he felt loved. If I surprised him with breakfast, or cleaned the house, or met him at work for coffee, he felt validated, seen, and special.

It is vital that we go beyond our preferred demonstration of love to tap into and meet our partners' needs.

We both respond to physical touch and frequently hold hands, give hugs and kisses, and cuddle. All relationships begin with areas of commonality and overlay that feel natural, meant to be, and easy. It's important to also be aware of how you may express love differently, which includes sexual appetites. Life circumstances change all the time, so how frequently you are sexually intimate may also flex and shift.

Throughout your life together, there may be times of forced abstinence: when a partner travels, during health issues such as surgery, illness, or childbirth, or other unforeseen circumstances. It's not something you're always thinking about when you are dating or engaged, but it is important to talk about as you consider your future together.

When Javi and I dated, we were used to being separated as he traveled about 50 percent of the time for work. This separation posed minimal hardship early on and even created romance in our relationship. But, over time, those experiences brought different circumstances and feelings. While I was perfectly fine when Javier traveled early on in our relationship, it became a struggle when he had to leave for an international business trip when our first daughter, Isabel, was only six days old. His absence was difficult, not just for sexual reasons, but emotionally. I was lonely and stressed, and when he returned, I had to warm up to being intimate. It took patience on both our parts to reunite emotionally as well as physically.

How your sex life changes throughout your marriage and how circumstances ebb and flow is important to recognize early on. Building the courage to talk about your expectations and needs with your partner builds intimacy and trust. We all go through periods of disillusionment and disappointment in our relationships. It is normal! And it does not mean that you are destined for a sexless and/or loveless marriage. The crucial part is to not assume that the frequency and intensity of sex will stay the same at any point in your relationship. Cultivate the safety and willingness to be vulnerable and talk about what you need.

I, personally, was shyer in talking about my sexuality and preferences in lovemaking. Javier was open, patient, and kind, and over time, I opened up, sharing what I needed and wanted. For many women, it is common to have felt forced or not respected in past sexual relationships. And, yes, men can also have these painful experiences. Bring those feelings to the table in marriage.

If you have been molested or abused and bury it, this can be a huge burden and source of pain, guilt, and shame that can unconsciously affect your sex life with your partner, even if it's amazing in the beginning in the relationship. Of course, seek the help you need, professionally or pastorally, but remember to honor your ever-changing needs.

Sex is a form of intimacy and an expression of unconditional love in a marriage. It needs to be consensual in all ways, and this is a standard that is important to hold up in every stage of your marriage. Our relationship heals us, and sometimes our sexual past does not come into play until years down the line.

Even when Javi watches our wedding video, he feels nostalgic and relives that special day. Romance is contagious. Like everything in life, we forget to remember that our partners are gifts from God. They are precious and uniquely crafted for our spiritual quest in life. We pray to hold onto this truth, regard our partner with reverence and devotion even when it's easy to take their presence in our life for granted.

Javier and I learned over time that a change in environment helped spark our sex life. By going on a trip or getting away for a weekend, Javier and I were able to reconnect and revisit our romance. By serving in our marriage preparation ministry, we were able to rekindle our courtship memories and relive those early experiences of adoration and desire.

> *We consciously created experiences to build closeness, taking us back to our courtship.*

Javier says that he marries me every year and he also courts me every year. With this perspective, we continually build upon our foundation of sexual intimacy and love.

The Dangers of Pornography
(JAVIER)

Growing up, my father and brother never spoke to me about sex. My sex education was based on interactions with my friends at school and conversations with my brother-in-law.

One day, my best friend decided we should put the VHS player he had in his room to good use. We visited the Video-Club (a retail store where you rent videos). We entered the store acting super casual, browsing through the action movie section and locating the XXX room. This room was in the back of the store, separated from the other VHS titles. As soon as we noticed that no one was watching, we snuck in to have a look.

We were totally shocked and could not make up our minds as to what to rent. We knew we had a very limited time to choose, so we picked a movie that didn't have a picture of a naked lady or a man on the cover. The store owner didn't care that we were minors at all. It was not until years later that I understood how the pornography industry works; they infiltrate children first, making them addicted to pornography.

That day, I was exposed to pornography for the first time. I watched the movie with a lot of surprise. And it began brainwashing me about what sex is and what intimacy looks like.

I was fourteen years old at the time, and that porno film was my first sex education class, which created faulty and misleading expectations of how men should behave. This all seems fairly innocent compared to the inappropriate content that is pushed via internet searches and online advertisements, but it was still destructive to my young mind.

Wherever the media is trying to capture an audience, pornography is there—on television, Netflix series, magazines, Instagram, and billboards. If advertisers want to catch your eye, they include a scantily clad woman on the ad. If a TV series wants to get your interest, they include sex scenes. If magazines want your money, a lot of beautiful women in sexy bikinis grace its pages. The list goes on. All offer some type of sexualized images. Every outlet that wants to capture your attention will offer some form of pornography.

Pornography affects the brain. Studies have found that the frequency of porn use correlates with depression, anxiety, stress, and social problems. It also affects your relationships. Pornography use has been found to influence some users' sexual preferences, leaving them wanting what they've seen onscreen and significantly less satisfied with sex in real life. Among the effects of the use of pornography is an increased negative attitude toward women, decreased empathy for victims of sexual violence, and an increase in dominating and sexually imposing behavior (https://fightthenewdrug.org).

Many popular films minimize infidelity, include unrealistic sex scenes, and depict betrayal as commonplace. People make mistakes, but our culture is fixated on the worst-case scenario and glorifies the drama.

Like many other men, I first learned about sex from pornography. Those images imprinted on my psyche. If it wasn't for my father directly teaching me how to treat a lady, I could have easily attracted someone with similar expectations about sex. I have been graced to know better and do better in my life.

Viewing the toxic images of pornography can definitely tempt you and destroy your marriage over time. Such unrealistic portrayals of sex and selfish desires can encourage infidelity. Relying on unhealthy images can lead to dissatisfaction in your relationship, prompting frustration, anger, and disillusionment.

It is vital to be open with each other and share your values and beliefs about sex before marriage. Get to know your future spouse on that level. Sex is not everything, but it needs to be discussed. Due to childbirth, sickness, business trips, and especially your kids growing up around you, your sex life will shift. Intimacy needs to be expressed in different ways, not just through sexual contact. Once we start that conversation openly with one other, we find ways to be intimate and better understand our partner's needs.

Relearning Intimacy

(JAVIER)

When I met Christina, I was thirty-three years old. I was open about my sexuality, and I invited her to have a conversation with me. She was reserved about sex, but I kept trying to have a dialogue in a fun, genuine, and understanding way. Humor was key. When I made Christina laugh about sex, her guard went down. This helped the topic of sex become less taboo for her, and have less power over both of us.

I traveled frequently during our first years of marriage, so we stayed connected during my business trips via phone. Having healthy, non-judgmental, and compassionate conversations about our sexual needs and expectations strengthened our relationship. I was open about my attraction for her and she slowly voiced her attraction for me while I was away.

Christina's first childbirth experience was grueling on her body. She was in labor for sixty-eight hours! I have never drunk so much coffee in my life. I wore a permanent smile with hospital staff and was beyond stressed. Our first daughter, Isabel Paulina, was born naturally, weighing 9.9 lbs. It took a huge toll on my wife's health. Christina left the hospital with a walker since she lost all sensation on her right side from her waist down. Her recovery was slow and difficult, especially with a newborn to care for.

We learned during that time how to be more intimate than ever. We understood that intimacy was not about having sex all the time. It was about reaching out with compassion to your future spouse and expressing your love by hugging, kissing, and using encouraging words.

> *A lot of men miss the boat when they don't realize that intimacy can be expressed by washing dishes, folding laundry, and even putting the toilet seat down.*

Yes, you heard me. Put on those yellow washing gloves and get ready to dig into the sink! Believe me, there is nothing sexier than a man doing the laundry and folding clothes for a woman.

Praying to our God for our spouse's well-being, strength, and happiness and for her to have courage is also a form of intimacy. When you go to God with your partner on your heart, He hears you. He blesses you both.

Christina and I supported each other through the babyhood of our first daughter who needed to be fed every three hours. Our communication grew and we truly understood how to be intimate in a situation where sex was not an option.

If you (men) were brought up like me, watching pornography and thinking that the only way to have intimacy is through sex, try to let go of those images and expectations. Marriage will force you to rewrite those guidelines. After childbirth, a woman needs to heal, and it is a huge life change at home. Sharing such a powerful experience redefines intimacy and sex. You will learn to love your wife in a new dimension.

There are so many more ways to express your love for your future wife in an intimate way. Be open, communicate, and let go of what you have learned. The norm is not always the right thing. We live in a society where the media taints our vision of what God is delivering to us. God loves us unconditionally and asks us to share a new kind of love with our spouse. I always like to think that the way we love others is the way we love ourselves internally.

Reflect on:

1) *How comfortable are you talking about sex with your partner? Can you share what you like, dislike, and what you are uncomfortable with?*

2) *What are your expectations about the intensity and frequency of sexual activity once you are married? Be honest and share your thoughts.*

3) *How do you feel about forced periods of abstinence? How do you feel about hearing "No" from your partner?*

CHAPTER 9

Financial Health

*"He who loves money will not be satisfied
with money, nor he who loves wealth
with his income; this also is vanity."*

—Ecclesiastes 5:10 (ESV)

Any Plan Is Better Than No Plan

(CHRISTINA)

Our discernment in prayer around finances and life goals boosted our prayer life as a couple. Many times, Javi and I mind mapped and did a deep analysis of our finances. Until we started praying over our finances and surrendering our fears of scarcity and failure to God, we ended up having a power struggle over money. Money has been a big hurdle for us as a couple, not in that we did not have it, but in how we managed it, organized it, and talked about it. So much of our childhood

161

fears around scarcity played into our money mindsets, so much so that we almost became different people when talking about it together.

I came from a financially privileged background in that my parents paid for my college, and I did not have to worry about money, food on the table, or any basic needs as a kid. Money was not a stressor and that was a huge gift in my life. My family went on vacation, and I lived in an upper-class neighborhood and attended excellent public schools. I played outside with friends in our Midwestern neighborhood. I felt safe, and I certainly never felt discriminated against due to my ethnic background or the color of my skin. I played sports, took part in clubs, and my parents were extremely financially supportive of my academics. They even helped me pay rent in NYC when I was in graduate school and always encouraged me in my ambitions and career goals.

When I entered my marriage, I was not financially savvy, even though I was employed, saved for retirement, worked, and paid my own bills. I was "adulting," but I paid little attention to my financial needs, let alone goals. I put extra earnings toward yoga classes, spiritual retreats, and travel to see friends. It was a fairly carefree life, and I only occasionally feared not having enough money to survive. I had a couple of breakdowns at tax time, but overall, I was doing "fine." In the back of mind, I knew that my family would not let me starve. This was a blessing, but it also served as an unconscious crutch. Overall, I did not have a vision of financial security or an idea of what it would take to raise a family in a financial sense. Despite living in two of the most expensive places in the United States (New York City and San Francisco), I was naive about money.

Javier had a very different upbringing with much more emotional and financial hardship, specifically when forging his way as a young adult. He worked from a very young age out of necessity, not out of luxury or to earn pocket money. Losing his parents young, he moved to the United States in middle school with no English. He paid rent to family members starting at age sixteen, worked throughout high school, and did all the household chores. At nineteen, he left his brother's home and financially struggled to pay rent and college tuition while waiting tables and working for the family business. His goal was to keep the electricity and phone bill paid. We came from opposite backgrounds in many ways. Little did we know the impact this would have on our marriage.

When we entered our engagement, Javi had financial debt accrued from a failed business, and I was finishing paying off my graduate student loan. We had little combined savings and it could not have felt more overwhelming and intimidating. Yet, I did not flinch. Perhaps this was denial, innocence, or just blind love. Javi seemed very fiscally responsible and aware. He came clean about this debt, and I had no doubt that we would eliminate being in the red *together*.

Overcoming Financial Fears

(CHRISTINA)

Despite this unconditional trust, I was hesitant to morph our checking and savings accounts. Clearly, I had some fear of losing control of my own money. It took us several "Come to Jesus" conversations and many books to figure out that if we truly believed in a faith-filled marriage, we had to learn to trust one another fully—no back doors, no secret or side accounts. We piled it all together and created joint checking and savings accounts. We had to come at it full force, with a merged financial ledger, into the marriage.

We knew that in our union, it was the right choice to combine finances. In some cases, couples may choose to keep finances separate for various business or personal reasons, but no matter what, finances shouldn't be a place of secrets, power plays, or manipulation. Money matters. Its vital energy in life and it can wreak havoc on any marriage at any stage of the game. In fact, money stress is one of the most cited conflicts that leads to separation, breakups, and divorce.

And with good reason. Money was a pothole for us during dating. We were completely unaware of our money mindsets or our inner fears of not having enough. Javi brought a significant amount of debt into our marriage, and we felt pressured to knock it out as soon as possible. We wanted that financial monkey off our back. We also lived in the extremely expensive Bay Area—an environment where material success is common, gentrification is ongoing, and the average home costs well over a million dollars.

To be honest, we have struggled every year with financial goals and reality. We talk openly about needing the freedom to buy a shirt or get a pedicure but also making sure that we are not doing this behind each other's backs. We learned to communicate before making purchases over $100 and still do. Transparency is key.

When Javi and I co-facilitate marriage preparation retreats, money remains one of the most taboo topics and also the most popular. We understand it is a frightening subject and can become a desperate issue for many people in and out of marriage. Folks often shyly approach us about our book recommendations and questions about our rocky path. I have learned that financial fidelity is similar to sexual fidelity—enter marriage with full disclosure and no secrets. This is a spiritual take on combining assets and debts:

Go all in to receive the blessings of a united bounty.

Early on in our marriage, we avoided putting zero percent down on a home to become "house poor" because we felt it would put too much stress on our marriage. Despite feeling pressured to take the plunge, we followed our gut and discerned with prayer. After doing the math on a dinner napkin one Sunday after church, Javi and I looked at each other and realized that money stress could drive us apart. We did not want to end up as a statistic—as another divorced couple.

Right then and there, we opted to rent a home (instead of buying one) which turned out to be an excellent choice. Our landlord lowered our rent quickly after we moved in as we were excellent tenants and the rent itself was a bargain in an extremely expensive area. We ended up saving more money than we could have if we bought a home and felt more security and flexibility in our finances. It was not an easy choice, but going to God in prayer helped us identify what was most important—keeping our marriage in a healthy place versus being homeowners.

I quickly learned that Javi received higher pay than me and merging our accounts actually brought more financial security into my life. I did not feel that I had to make it all alone, and I had a partner, not only spiritually and emotionally, but also in the creation of a future in the material world. We certainly understand that this is a personal choice, but we strongly encourage people to talk about their money fears, expectations, concerns, and limits. We are not experts but have simply learned that financial transparency early on brings grace in good and hard times with money. We are no strangers to the fact that money issues can trigger one's core fears and hidden worries.

Owning Your Financial Future

(CHRISTINA)

It can be uncomfortable, even awkward at first, to check in so frequently about money, but it's made us stronger and more accountable in our finances. By sharing our financial dreams and desires, we also learned to reassess our priorities and distinguish our wants from our needs. Even now, we pray before we head into financial discussions because control issues and fears come up easily. It's a lifelong learning process, but we have learned to face it head-on.

Our honesty, prayer, and discernment have gotten us through periods of minimal cash flow in businesses, unemployment, employers going bankrupt, sudden layoffs, and even lawsuits. We're not trying to scare you, but we seriously had no idea of the financial challenges that were ahead of us when we were engaged.

You cannot always prepare for the obstacles that you will face in life, but you can certainly hone the skills (prayer and communication) to help weather the storms and provide hope.

We have found that the key to building a financially sound marriage is putting everything on the table early and laying out a mind map or at least a list of how you want to spend, save, tithe (give), and share. It doesn't have to include the "B" word (the dreaded budget), but it certainly means that you need to look at your total debt, assets, and income together frequently.

Again, you may want to keep separate accounts and just one shared account, and you may have more complicated finances than we did when we started out. The trap is assuming that financial issues will "just work their way out" without active and consistent discussions. For us, getting over the fear of not having enough or not contributing enough has been a process. We are constantly growing and changing in our careers and lifestyles. So it's important to continually assess our priorities and talk about our saving and spending.

Fear will rear it's big, ugly head over and over again. Make friends with it. It's trying to protect you and your relationship. Pray over your money, find gratitude for what you have (even if it doesn't feel like enough), give to causes and sources that move you, and review your bottom line together. Anything is possible with God, so remember there is no money mountain or debt pinnacle that you cannot climb and conquer.

> *"Money is an opportunity to reach unity in marriage. When couples work together, they can do anything."*
>
> —DAVE RAMSEY

Javi and I have paid off tens of thousands of dollars of debt, and we are still standing, taller and prouder for it. Do we still have growing pains about finances? Absolutely! But growth is what marriage is all about. So dive in deep and get to the bottom line of your financial relationship. You will reap the benefits more than you can possibly imagine.

The Burden of Debt

(JAVIER)

Every time I think of financial health, I think of Wells Fargo Bank. Not because of their marketing tactics, horse wagon, customer service, or how many locations they have compared to Starbucks. I think of that first credit card that I was invited to have set up at the college I was attending. My approval took a while since internet back then was not as speedy as it is today, but in two weeks I got my answer. "Hello, Mr. Llerena, you have been granted an $800-dollar line of credit."

Oh, boy! The first purchase was a music CD and it felt so good. Now, I didn't have to have money to buy things. I was happy for a short period of time. I felt free financially. I felt that I could bring that satisfaction ten times more if I made an even larger purchase. I went on dates and literally maxed out that $800. I think the girls who went out with me must have thought it was an amazing date with a fool of a dude who was ordering food like it was his last meal. When I maxed out my card, they magically increased my credit limit to $1200 USD. Guess what I did? I bought a CD player that cost me exactly $400 to top off that new limit.

∽

That was the beginning of my debt journey. I became addicted to credit cards, retail store cards, and loans. I also failed to file my taxes on time. Additionally, I worked with my brother and was self-employed. I didn't bother filing those taxes at all at first, which brought my debt into a snowball. From there, the debt grew from $15K, $25K, $35K, to a maximum of $75K. I remember that the deeper I got into debt, the more I borrowed to pay the debts back—a vicious cycle. I learned the hard way about the credit predators. I learned how harsh and persistent collection agencies can be. The blinking light on my answering machine back then would always burn out due to the number of collection agencies calling me, leaving threatening messages.

My credit reports were a horror story. I avoided them for years. I had negative collection notations. At the lowest, my FICO score was 200. It was like a debt snowball from one collection agency to the next, and I was lost under the weight of making poor financial decisions as a young adult.

Accruing a lot of debt was not an overnight process; it took close to fourteen years. I simply didn't have the financial education that every young person should before they get a part-time job and start playing with real money. My brother, who raised me, never taught me about finances or how to manage your money. My money management skills were so out of whack that even when I used management helps like Quicken, I didn't have the skills to make the most of them. I had Quicken for years and all I did was enter data. I didn't establish a budget or try to cut the debt.

The worst part of being in debt is that you tend to surrender to the fact that you will never crawl out of the debt. I would fantasize every day that I would win the lottery or the debt would miraculously be forgiven. That didn't occur; my management skills didn't improve and the debt got bigger. The agony, frustration, and depression from such a large debt took up permanent residence in my heart.

Doing the Right Thing

(JAVIER)

When I met Christina, I was in one of the rebirth stages of my life. I built those internal and external boundaries that provided me the foundation for the greatest thing that I could do for myself: SELF-LOVE. I was loving myself, letting go of the situations that hurt me in the past, and controlling my destiny. My finances were one of those skeletons in the closet that I needed to solve fast. Otherwise, the internal boundaries that I created would serve no purpose. One day I yelled from the top of my lungs, "Enough is enough. There has to be a way to end all this messed up debt that I have created!"

The first step was that I took responsibility for all my actions. It was hard to do, but I was determined to move forward with a healthy financial plan. I didn't blame the IRS, Wells Fargo Bank, or even Comerica Bank for giving me a car loan with a 22 percent interest rate. I didn't blame my brother for not educating me about money or informing me that I needed to pay self-employment taxes. I owned the fact that I got myself in debt. I prayed to the Lord for solutions so I could make wise choices and erase my financial mistakes.

As it was, I stumbled into a book that changed my perspective and helped me take ownership of my finances: *The Debt-Free & Prosperous Living Basic Course* by John M. Cummuta. I believe the book is out of print, but it saved me. Thanks to that book, I tackled my debt issues head-on. I established a plan and knew that I was going to be out of debt soon. The book also provided me with what it took to change my belief system about money. The plan was in action, and I felt the weight being lifted from my back.

The topic of money will appear as a cameo in your dating life, and if you decided to move forward into the sacrament of marriage, it will play a larger role, one that you can't ignore. I was embarrassed at first thinking of how I was going to tell Christina that I was in a $75K pile of debt, that the IRS was on my tail for not paying back taxes, and that I didn't have a retirement plan. It was hard at first to explain the situation to her. I thought that she might leave and call off the wedding, but the wisdom of my dad tapped into me.

My dad always taught me that you marry for life until death. This includes in sickness or health, poverty or prosperity. I realized that I needed to be fully open about everything—money included. I decided to explain to Christina my situation and show her the plan I had put in place to eliminate it in less than twenty months.

I worked my plan and had proof that the debt was decreasing significantly each month. My credit rating moved up, and I was able to negotiate a payment plan with the creditor. I was proud that I could tell Christina and show her how everything was going to work out. In less than two years, I would be out of debt. And it happened! I was out of debt, building up my credit, and had a new, healthy relationship with money.

Unfortunately, the topic of finances is a common trigger for couples, and financial stress tears apart many relationships. Being financially healthy is to be honest in your relationship and expose where you are and where you want to go with money. Money is a vehicle, and if it is not driven properly you will have a bumpy ride. Be transparent with one another and have a plan on how you are going to manage your finances.

In the free companion workbook, there are examples and questions that will help you reflect and support you in having a healthy financial life together as a couple. There is nothing like combining your finances!

Reflect on:

1) What money issues do you have that you and your partner need to discuss?

2) Do you have any debt to pay off together? Do you know your financial goals for buying a home and/ or saving for retirement?

3) What is your biggest hope and dream for your financial future together?

4) What is your biggest obstacle that could get in the way of that financial dream coming to life?

CHAPTER 10

Forgiveness

"Let all bitterness and wrath and anger and clamor and slander be put away from you, along with all malice. Be kind to one another, tenderhearted, forgiving one another, as God in Christ forgave you."

—Ephesians 4:31-32 (ESV)

"In marriage, every day you love and every day you forgive. It's an ongoing sacrament, love, and forgiveness."

—Bill Moyers

"Marriage is three parts love and seven parts forgiveness of sins."

—Lao Tzu

Do You Want to Be Right or Forgiven?

(CHRISTINA)

One of my favorite comments (there are so many) from our younger daughter, Lucia, to our older daughter, Isabel, was during an argument when Isabel was rallying for her cause (she is extremely persistent and persuasive) and there happened to be a pause. Lucia asked, "Isabel, do you want to be right or do you want to be kind?" Bam! There it is. We all sat with that question for a split second.

We have a choice every day to be kind and generous with our partner. Sometimes, it's easy peasy, lemon squeezy. The love is there, it flows, all is well in the universe and you are divinely connected. Other times, it is like squeezing blood from a stone. You are bitter, angry, hurt, and cannot believe you know this person let alone have forgiven him/her for whatever he/she did this time. It's a cycle that can happen many times in one day or even one conversation. As spiritual beings, we are called to forgive "70 x 7" times, which is a reality beyond our scope.

We are called to be boundless in our forgiveness of one another as God has forgiven us again and again and again.

Preparing for marriage is gearing up for a forgiveness marathon. You can start or restart training at any time. Don't sweat it. It sucks at first, but you GOT this! If you are not in a relationship and desire one, practice forgiving yourself for the past and present. (This is also a healing practice if you are IN a relationship.) If you are in a relationship, ask for forgiveness from God, from yourself, and from your partner humbly and often.

One of the most powerful acts of grace is found in going to your spouse to acknowledge their recent sacrifices for you. With practice, Javier and I created a mutual habit to verbally thank one another for acts of service (putting clothes away, loading the dishwasher) that may not be over-the-top amazing but make an impact in our daily lives.

Forgiving the Unforgivable

(CHRISTINA)

Javier and I had worked through our cultural differences, our family baggage, and our financial stresses. We knew we loved each other, and we felt we were supposed to be together. We had chosen to follow God and to raise our family in faith. So everything should have been easy and perfect for us, right? Wrong! We were still human beings with some very big human failings. Life, and some of its inevitable obstacles, sometimes still brought out the worst in us.

∽

Our rock bottom episode came just after our second baby was born. I was suffering from significant postpartum depression. That was hard enough, but to make it more difficult, Javier refused to see how much I was struggling. Instead of being supportive, he felt rejected and alone. These feelings culminated on the night of his fortieth birthday.

He started drinking early (as did everyone else) and we became distanced throughout the night. People were pitching in to pay the dinner bill and he was furious—he does not believe that guests should pay the bill. This was the final trigger that tipped him off and made him furious.

He was seething inside and he began drinking more. I stopped drinking earlier and was already dreading how the night would end. By the time we got home, he promised his brother he would not do "anything," but the minute we entered the home, he became completely enraged. He began screaming, throwing things, breaking furniture. I ran from the dining room and locked myself in the bathroom, calling 911. Javier continued to rage until—worn out—he went to the garage.

The police came quickly. I left the bathroom and answered the door. They were reassuring and I realized that Javi had left the home. They gave me their card and encouraged me not to be alone. I called Javi's brother, and he came over right away. Isabel had woken up (she was almost four at the time). I packed our bags, scooped up the girls, and stayed with Javi's brother and family for the night. We returned late the next day.

When Javi came home that night, he slept in the guest room. He had to leave for a business trip the next day. While I was gone, I sought counsel from a lawyer who told me that I had a case and informed me on how to get a restraining order.

While away, Javier found out that I was considering legal action and he was devastated.

That first week, I slept with a cell phone under my pillow. This was grueling and humbling. I remember crying so much at times that my eyelids were swollen.

The turning point for me was during one of our conversations after the incident. Javi asked me point blank, "Do you still love me?"

I did not hesitate. My heart spoke for me. And I said unequivocally, "Yes." It was like a new wave of energy and strength entered our relationship from that moment on.

Javier said, "That's all I needed to hear."

That moment shifted us toward starting over. I believe it was a miracle moment guided by God. We sought counseling together, and Javier went to individual counseling as well.

Counseling took several months. I had to reconcile the man I loved (and love) with the man I feared that night. I had to face my role in our conflict and own my part in his emotional downfall. I did not take responsibility for his actions but realized that he did not act in a vacuum.

I vacillated from wanting to treat our marriage as a "domestic violence case" from my social work career and filing for a separation to collapsing in tears to our priest in total vulnerability to God. I remember going on my knees in prayer to God to ask for directions and clear insight on what to do.

After getting the insight I needed, I sought help for postpartum depression. I learned that my self-neglect had led to a collapse in our marriage. It was a turning point in my heart. I put the man I loved before the man I experienced that night. I turned to God for a miracle and surrendered my marriage to

Him. My willingness to forgive Javier saved our marriage, and I know that God performed a miracle in both hearts to help us heal and rebuild.

That said, we understand that all relationships are not salvageable. We share our rock bottom to show how bad things can get even when you love each other and are trying to do things right. However, there are women (and men) in severely abusive relationships. The abuser apologizes; the abused forgives. And then it happens again and again and again. These are relationships that should be left, especially if there are children involved. This is true, cyclical abuse.

We do not suggest putting forgiveness before personal safety. Professional help needs to be sought; family and friends and faith communities can also be huge assets in navigating these volatile situations. Javier's willingness to change and my willingness to work with him were key components of our unique situation.

As fallible, imperfect humans, we recognize our many weaknesses. We know that we are extremely fortunate and blessed to have healed and moved past intimidation and violence in our relationship. It was hard work seeking and receiving help and committing to one another without knowing the outcome. The grace of God truly pulled us through.

Forgiveness is not about letting bygones be bygones or getting over it. It is about seeing what is given when you do not deserve it. Your partner gives to you at times when you are not necessarily worthy and this boundless reciprocity is the key to forgiving intentionally and often. This can be about big things or small things, but the ability to forgive paves the way for boundless love to flourish and surpass your expectations in your marriage.

Clean the Basement First

(Javier)

Before you can forgive someone, you need to forgive yourself. If we don't forgive fully we are carrying all those feelings inside of us. Yes, holding a grudge makes us feel safe and gives us a reason to be angry, frustrated, and even "right." But all this does is create more pain inside us as we project the worst of us to the outside world.

My opinion used to be that anger is a good thing to have for a short while. But holding onto anger is like carrying poison inside of you. The longer it lingers inside, the more damage it causes and the longer it takes to heal. The anger can be caused by something you did that made you feel horrible about yourself and so you became angry with yourself.

Anger was a mechanism that I saw in action very vividly while growing up with my dad. He used it to intimidate people or to forcefully communicate when things were not going his way. As I stated in the previous paragraphs, the poison you bottle up inside needs to come out some way or another. It can exit in bad ways—through food, alcohol, drugs, promiscuous sex, or any type of addiction.

Personally, I suffered from a lack of anger management. And I don't mean that I just raised my voice sometimes. In the first years of my marriage, breaking private property was my outlet. This was often combined with alcohol use. It is common for anger and booze to go hand in hand. I should point out that even in my most terrible behavior, I never threatened Christina.

It was like the alcohol provided an open ticket to behave badly, break private property, and explode with anger. It felt good at the moment, like a cloud of steam was finally released out of me. Immediately after, a horrible feeling would take over, and I would feel a deep sadness and a sense of abandonment.

This had been a habit of mine for a while. I experienced many of these angry episodes throughout my dating life. I would always excuse them and when I got over the horrible feeling of sadness and abandonment, I would forget about it. When I dated Christina, I thought I was past the worst of it. I didn't realize that the anger was building up more and more. No matter the person or relationship, the rage and the pain were still inside of me.

Rude Awakening

(JAVIER)

The worst incident was during my fortieth birthday. It should have been a wonderful, celebratory night, but in my mind, I was turning forty years old. Instead of a festive celebration, that night was like a 4th of July fireworks display of anger.

Everything that was bottled inside of me exploded like a champagne cork from an open bottle. My wife was going through postpartum depression and I ignored it. When she was just really exhausted and depressed, I felt that she was ignoring and rejecting me during my birthday celebration. I felt unloved and unacknowledged. This triggered my past trauma of rejection and abandonment.

Christina was very distanced from me during that time, dealing with a toddler and a new baby, but I took it personally. In reality, she was reacting from her symptoms of depression. Looking back, I didn't understand her depression for years.

As soon as I stepped into the house with Christina, my rage took over. I felt out of control with my feelings of abandonment and rejection. I began to scream and swear. I broke the furniture in my house that I deeply loved. I scared my two daughters, and I terrified my wife so badly that she locked herself in the bathroom with the girls and called 911.

After I felt exhausted from breaking furniture, yelling, and crying my eyes out, I headed toward the garage. I had a movie playing in my head that as soon as I opened the garage, I was going to meet the cops. They would arrest me in front of my family and that would be the end of my misery.

Well, God works in strange ways! The cops got there literally three minutes after I left the house. I wandered around the neighborhood crying my eyes out. I was heartbroken. I was scared that I would lose my family. I felt disappointed and ashamed of myself. As I was walking, I thought that the cops were looking for me and would eventually arrest me. But that didn't happen.

The police came and left right before my brother arrived. Since I broke private property and threatened my wife, the police gave Christina an option to arrest me if she felt in danger. She didn't move forward with the arrest.

My brother, Miguel, helped calm the situation and took Christina and my two daughters with him to his house. I later returned to the house and cleaned up my mess. I contemplated the broken furniture, got down on my knees and prayed to the

Lord for help. I packed a bag and headed to a hotel nearby. I reflected and sobered up the next couple of days before returning home. I needed help in significant doses!

We remained living in the same house for our girls, but I slept in our spare bedroom temporarily. I attended individual counseling, and we went to couples counseling for several months. We each spoke with our priest separately. We prayed, she prayed, and I prayed. I realized that all the anger I had brewing inside of me was due to watching my father be so bitter and mean in different situations of my life.

I will never forget when my dad asked me what I wanted to be when I grew up. For some reason, I wanted to be a parachuter for the Spanish army. I thought to myself that jumping out of planes was the coolest thing. He would laugh and tell me derisively that I could never accomplish that—the only thing that I would achieve in my life was to be a bouncer at a nightclub. I am 5' 8" and 160 pounds, so who knows how I was going to achieve that?!

I eventually became aware that my unresolved anger from childhood was rooted in unhealed pain from the past. A multitude of traumas impacted me and I had not fully faced the emotional impact. The abuse at the orphanage, my father's rage, and the loss of both my parents by the age of thirteen, on top of moving to a foreign country, caused much suffering in my teenage years. Until I recognized my pain, I could not fully heal myself.

I overlooked that anger. It fueled me to move forward in my life so I could emotionally survive, but there was only so much that my mind, soul, and heart could take. I was extremely resilient, but there was a limit to what I could hold inside.

Eventually, it spilled out, taking over my life. I now think anger is the root of all evil.

I learned how to forgive. I chose to fully forgive my father because I know now that he was dealing with so much pain. He carried pain from his childhood all the way to his last day. This was pain that he didn't know how to channel into something positive.

Moreover, I hoped that Christina would forgive me. After some time, much counseling, and a change in my behaviors, she did. We began by respecting each other's feelings and space. "One step at a time" was my mantra every day. The only thing that was in my mind was to keep my family together. I realized that I needed healing. It wasn't so much about my wife or myself being right or wrong, but us working to have a great marriage again. Many individual and couple therapy sessions added better communication between us. It was time to learn more about myself and start the healing process. I felt Christina's forgiveness and the mercy of God in her actions. In my heart, I knew that we would get another start.

As months progressed, we started to connect on a deeper level. I kept working on myself and understanding how to control myself. I would reflect on where the anger was coming from, make peace with it and identify the triggers so I could reflect on them in time. I also understood my wife's depression and anxiety. I educated myself and supported her. I didn't see it as a weakness in her but something that we should be aware of. We all have some degree of depression or anxiety at different points in our lives.

We decided to celebrate our fifth wedding anniversary and renew our vows. I chose the first Christian church in Kona,

Hawaii. I even hired a photographer to capture the celebration. We have the pictures displayed at our house, and as the years pass, the more I realize what it meant for us. It was a moment of rebirth. This time we were stronger than ever.

Reflect on:

1) *Are you holding onto anything that happened in the past that could be blocking your love for your partner?*

2) *Are you willing to forgive easily and often? Why or why not?*

3) *If you are holding a grudge, can you pray to let it go to God?*

4) *If you know that you have failed your partner in some way, are you able to take a moment to acknowledge the sin, take responsibility, and ask them for forgiveness? Are you able to take the steps that will cause a long-term change in your behavior?*

CHAPTER 11

Your Ideal Marriage

"Always be humble, gentle, and patient, accepting each other in love. You are joined together with peace through the Spirit, so make every effort to continue together in this way."

—Ephesians 4:2-3 (ESV)

Preparation Matters

(CHRISTINA)

Marriage is the biggest emotional and spiritual investment of your lifetime. However, it is more than that. It is tempting to forget how much we need to "save" before entering marriage. We start by loving ourselves and growing our faith and relationship with God. Then we begin to build trust, forgiveness, and hope in order to become "marriage material."

We cannot give what we do not have. When we prepare emotionally and spiritually, we still hit obstacles, challenges, and crises, but we are more able to navigate through those rocky times. When we leverage our faith in our life and our marriage, we are open to seeing a bigger picture, a larger perspective beyond the immediate pain that makes us stronger and more resilient as individuals and as a couple.

This emotional and spiritual preparation provides a necessary foundation for a healthy and spiritually-sound relationship with our partner for years to come. How much time and energy we spend in preparation will directly correlate to what kind of marriage we lead. When you invest in a relationship, you nurture it, give it love, and hold it dear.

You make large financial purchases over time usually by saving and/or earning more money and then paying it off in installments or even taking out a loan to pay the "good debt" back. It can be a lifelong process and your investment gives back to you in many ways throughout your life. Marriage transcends these terms. It never gets paid off but it gives back to you more than you can ever imagine.

Our society perpetuates myths of romance, lust, and passion without holding up examples of loyalty, trust, and commitment. Marriage can be viewed as a confusing proposition in that its core promises are not held up or cherished in our world. Our concept and "vision" of marriage is tainted from the start. We must unlearn and release these negative messages our society has ingrained in us in order to bring into manifestation the truth of what our marriage can be.

It is so vital to wake up to yourself, your values, and your relationship in life to fully prepare for the lifetime commitment of marriage. The more we can identify who we are and what we really, really want, the more likely our relationship will be fulfilling, lasting, and a vehicle for our personal growth.

By embracing self-respect, self-love, and worthiness in God's eyes, we open ourselves to a new version of marriage— one that loves unconditionally, sees friendship and sacrifice as part of God's gift and constantly pushes us to grow in ways that we never fathomed before.

Make Your Marriage Your Masterpiece

(CHRISTINA)

Consider entering your marriage with an intentional, co-created vision of what kind of relationship you want, who you both want to be, and what you wish, desire, and hope for one another. Temporal goals are great, but what spiritual or moral values do you want to embody together? Where do you see yourselves in 5, 10, 20 years? How might you give back to the world together? This intentionality makes all the difference because you have a road map, a template of what you want, and a map on how to get there. Yes, it will twist, turn, and morph as you go, so consider it a working draft.

Javier and I have used mind maps, countless post-it papers, and vision boards to map out our goals and individual projects. This may sound over the top but it's how we stay on track and keep moving toward the future—together. Over time, we have learned that Javier is visual and needs to see things written out on a whiteboard or big paper. I need notes, a document to refer to so I can check items off and remember.

When you pray over your dreams together, God hears you and wants to empower you. Seek out ways to be grateful for what you have together so your progress is acknowledged and your marriage is grounded. One of the most beautiful things about sharing your marriage with God is discovering the twists and turns and open doors that He has for you.

> *"We grow in time to trust the future for our answers."*
>
> — RUTH BENEDICT

Hold up your future to God so it may be blessed. Remember that He is using your relationship to exemplify love and magnify it. Don't be that couple who walks unconsciously through life together because that is what you were taught or have seen around you. Life is too challenging, too deep, and too fulfilling to not take the time to ask some basic questions of what do we want to create together.

A Lifetime Celebration

(JAVIER)

When Christina and I were planning our wedding, we learned that weddings are a massive industry and lucrative business. In the United States, the average couple spends $33,000 on their wedding (https://money.cnn.com/2018/01/16/pf/wedding-cost/index.html). This can range from destination weddings to big galas to inviting everyone in your life as well as some people you may not have even met!

Planning a wedding can be very stressful, time-consuming, and confusing. There are many opportunities for the wedding industry to pursue you to purchase, contract, and pay a lot of money without really looking out for your best interests. Also, the process loses sight of the true meaning of what marriage means by focusing on the "party" and "politics" versus the spiritual transformation at stake.

When Christina and I walked into a Wedding Expo, we were shocked at the amount of money we could invest in one single day. Often, we, as a culture, invest so much in one big day, one big celebration, but we lose sight of our long-term goals.

A marriage is much more than a one-day celebration or party. It is a vow of a lifetime—of unconditional love, sacrifice, self-growth, and parenting. Without a plan, your marriage will likely take you places that you didn't plan.

Over the years of facilitating in our ministry of San Jose Engaged Encounter, we see the joy and excitement of the couples when they discuss their wedding plan. It is super exciting! But when we ask the planning questions about their future, we notice that those goals are less clear in their minds.

Marriage, like parenting, doesn't come with a user manual. Yes, you will get tons of advice from your parents, relatives, and friends on how you should do things with your spouse. Keep in mind that they are speaking from their experiences. Every marriage is a unique union of love. The only one who is all-knowing is God.

Marriage is for life, the biggest commitment that you are going to make. And like everything else in life, you don't want to make a commitment without having a plan.

A Pioneer's Journey

(JAVIER)

If you don't know where you want to be, it will be harder to get there. Over the years, my wife and I have been facilitating for San Jose Engaged Encounter and we see many in love, excited couples eagerly anticipating their big wedding day. They are consumed by the details: flowers, cake, invitations, the bridal party, family expectations, etc. They are very focused on the wedding and not their marriage.

They worry more about the color of the tablecloths than how they plan to deal with relatives over the holidays. Since Christina and I have been facilitating Catholic Engaged retreats, we always get asked what the secret to a great marriage is.

The truth is that there are no shortcuts or quick fixes in marriage, but your faith can work miracles. Marriage is a process of both people moving toward, investing, loving, and relying on faith in God for hope, Fatherly love, and wisdom. God holds all the answers. He is so eager to know your plan, not just a hidden agenda, but your plan as a couple.

When we realize some of the powerful gifts we have with God on our side, it becomes easier and more satisfying to plan a God-centered life together. Christina and I are both planners by nature. During our Catholic Engaged retreat, we took our future planning very seriously. We looked at how we were going to spend the holidays and how we wanted to raise our children. We wanted our kids to have a faith-based environment and we even tackled my financial debt to create a recovery plan and decided to merge our financial accounts.

The planning process was better than I expected. I went as far as trying to open a 529 college fund for my first daughter without her being born! The bank politely told me to come back with our child's birth certificate after she had arrived. We both had vision boards and dreams of being physically fit and healthy, purchasing a house, investing in mutual funds, and enjoying life together.

One key element was missing, though. Sometimes I forgot to include God in our decision-making process. It was easy to get tangled up in all the details. I was so busy doing financial, faith, family arrangements, and health planning that I missed connecting with God and seeing what He had in mind for us. I momentarily overlooked our values, beliefs, and customs as a couple.

Reflect on:

1) *What is our overall vision for family life and our family? What is most important to each of us?*

2) *What goals could we set that will help us achieve this vision?*

3) *Are there any conflicts between the two visions we have for family life? Why do they exist? Is either of us willing to compromise?*

4) *How will we support each other through our academic, professional, and family life?*

5) *How will we share and/or divide household labor?*

6) *How can we play different roles in the family but still maintain an equal partnership?*

CONCLUSION

"When I was a child, I spoke like a child, I thought like a child, I reasoned like a child. When I became a man, I gave up childish ways. For now we see in a mirror dimly, but then face to face. Now I know in part; then I shall know fully, even as I have been fully known. So now faith, hope, and love abide, these three; but the greatest of these is love"

—1 Corinthians 13: 11-13 (ESV)

JAVIER AND I WROTE THIS book to share our story and spiritual journey as a couple to inspire others to put God at the center of their relationship in preparing for marriage. We have learned and relearned this lesson through our time together. We are humbled and broken and united for it. This book is for anyone preparing for marriage: single, coupled, or engaged. Its focus is on God as the center of the relationship above all.

We journeyed from loving oneself to identifying and maintaining healthy boundaries to knowing who we are and who we are not as individuals. Each of these steps is crucial and intentional in building a marriage that transcends life's difficulties and challenges. These are the lessons of early adulthood and dating that form us and inform our choices in relationships. Looking critically and thoughtfully at dating leads us to a better model of courtship based on mutual respect, transparency, and commitment.

A key factor of our message is putting God at the center of your relationship early on, before marriage. When you pray for your perfect partner, trust that God has a plan and He will not only bring your mate to you but bless you both as you grow in your relationship with Him. Lean on your faith in God to guide your decisions and prepare yourselves for a lifetime of parallel spiritual growth, especially embracing the lifelong work of forgiveness.

"There is no more lovely, friendly and charming relationship, communion or company than a good marriage."

—Martin Luther

To get here, we shared how this can mean deeply questioning what we learned about dating, commitment, marriage, sex, and intimacy from our past and society at large. This can also mean reflecting on our childhood, our family, past relationships, and examining our beliefs about love, marriage, and commitment. This takes courage and we commend you.

We know this journey can be scary and sometimes unpopular. It is not easy to have hard conversations, face your feelings, and own your mistakes. Sometimes, it may feel much safer to keep your head down, ignore the signs and patterns in your life, and live unaware of the choices you make as well as their consequences. Our mission is to share with you that by opening your heart and mind to God, amazing goodness and growth awaits.

We know how hard it is. We know the pain. We know the loneliness. We know the gravity of our own mistakes. But we know that there is also hope, healing, and redemption. We have faced crises in our own marriage and have come out of them by putting God at the center of our struggle, our decisions, and fundamentally, our marriage. When you trust in God, love never ends.

"We are here to love. Not much else matters."

— FRANCIS CHAN

We know personally that God strengthens and fortifies our marriage every day. We would be nothing without Him but lost and broken. Our faith inspires us to be better and bigger than who we naturally are as humans. Through Christ's love as his daughter and son, we are moved to transcend our sin, our shame, and our past mistakes. We forgive, laugh, atone, repent, and surrender.

Our prayer is that you build a faith-based foundation with your beloved and enter a marriage that grows and exceeds all your expectations of what you think love is and can be. We pray that your love becomes *boundless*, more than anything you could ever have imagined or experienced in your life.

Thank you for reading our story. We offered it humbly to you, knowing that miracles await your relationship with God at your side. May you remember your worth in His eyes, see your partner as He sees him or her, and cherish the moments of beauty that are before you now and forevermore. That you both will have truly, boundless love.

In Him,

Christina & Javier

WANT TO GO FURTHER?

WE ENCOURAGE YOU, THE READER, to actively create a vision for your future marriage. It doesn't matter if you are single and seeking a mate or have dated your partner for a long time, this is a powerful effort to usher in change and growth in your life.

Taking time to pray and intentionally envision and design your future brings greater awareness of and appreciation for your life. By inviting the Holy Spirit to guide us, our relationships deepen and our strengths and talents magnify. It is our birthright as children of God to have a life that brings healing into our lives.

When you consciously plan your future, you pave the road for your deepest intentions to be fulfilled and deepen your relationship by opening yourself to Boundless Love. In our workshops, we create a deeper conversation with prayer, reflection, and a dialogue of inquiry that leads to a reassuring connection with God and your future.

Throughout the year, we offer workshops for individuals and couples who want to prepare for marriage and/or revitalize their relationships. These are for singles who are preparing their hearts for their divine partner to show up in their lives. They are also for couples who are discerning if marriage is the next step, and for those who are engaged and spiritually preparing for marriage. Our prayer is that you each feel God's grace in taking the next step in your relationship with Him and each other.

To find out more about our workshops for individuals and couples, please go to our website at www.boundlesslove.us.

RESOURCES

WE WANT TO LEAVE YOU with books, events, and media that inspired us and enhanced our marriage preparation journey. We truly hope that you find a "gem" in here where God shows you exactly what you needed at the perfect time. Enjoy!

- *There Is Nothing Wrong with You*, by Cheri Huber
- *The Five Love Languages*, by Gary Chapman
- *You Can Heal Your Life*, by Louise Hay
- *Jesus Calling*, by Sarah Young
- *Radical Forgiveness*, by Colin Tipping
- *The Miracle Morning*, by Hal Elrod
- *The Miracle Morning for Couples*, by Hal Elrod and Lance and Brandy Salazar
- *The Front Row Factor*, by Jon Vroman
- *Living Forward*, by Michael Hyatt and Daniel Harkavy
- *Rhinoceros Success*, by Scott Alexander
- *Resisting Happiness*, by Mathew Kelly
- *The Total Money Makeover*, by Dave Ramsey
- *Life Over Coffee podcast*, by Rick Thomas

- *The SeedTime Living podcast*, by Bob Lotich
- *Best Year Ever* [Blueprint] Live Event
- *Front Row Summit Live Event*

CONVERSATIONS FOR EXPONENTIAL OUTCOMES

About the Flourishing Leadership Institute and the XCHANGE Training and Certification

HOW DO COUPLES, LEADERS, ENTREPRENEURS, and change agents (managers, consultants, trainers, coaches, speakers, facilitators) enable a relationship, team, community, or organization to come alive, be at its very best... achieve outcomes that matter most... more naturally, effectively, and faster than ever before? We have never known as much as we do today in our collective search for the answers to this question.

The Flourishing Leadership Institute (FLI) is the leading global provider of Appreciative Inquiry Large Group Summits and exclusive provider of the XCHANGE Training and Certification used by leaders of all kinds (from leaders of families to global organization). Learn more at https://www.lead2flourish.com/training

The **XCHANGE Training and Certification** offers a proven answer to this question and approach for an emergent group of "leader facilitators" who recognize the collective calling for a dramatically new "approach to leadership" built around the ability to:

- Lead groups to design and facilitate questions and "conversations worth having" that elicit and draw upon individual and collective strengths, deepen engagement, co-create shared values, purpose, vision, and action
- Enable complex strategic change, not only in individuals, but also at the scale of the whole system (relationship, family, team, organization, community)

...and do all of this more rapidly, naturally and effectively than ever before!

XCHANGE participants learn how to apply the "leadership operating system" that FLI uses to facilitate cultural transformations, strategic planning, leadership development, community building, and whole system change that has been used with clients like BMW, TEDx, and Facebook

The XCHANGE approach draws from a convergence of evidence based sciences and practices including Appreciative Inquiry, Neuroscience, Strengths-based Leadership, Positive Psychology, Biomimicry, Sustainable Value Creation, Emotional Intelligence, Experiential Learning, Adaptive Holistic Facilitation, SOAR, and more.

ABOUT THE FLOURISHING LEADERSHIP INSTITUTE

The six-month training is an immersive and experiential journey that starts with a five day in-person. The training also includes a series of virtual trainings (live video coaching and deeper trainings on XCHANGE components), peer-to-peer and applied learning experiences. Participants gain access to FLI's intellectual property (e.g. engagement agendas, workbooks... even proposals) using the XCHANGE approach with its own clients. A prerequisite is all participants have specific and immediate opportunities to apply the training, ensuring the learning journey is practical and impactful.

One of the most valuable aspects of the XCHANGE journey is our engaged community of lifelong learning partners. Participants benefit from ongoing pee- to- peer learning inspired by the direct application of the XCHANGE Approach across a diversity of environments and geographies. Our most recent class included participants from Dubai, Germany, Great Britain, Denmark, France, Canada, Mexico, and all across the U.S.

> *"XCHANGE has been attracting an amazing group of superstars. The work that I see them (FLI) doing in the large group planning sphere, is probably some of the best AI summits and planning processes that I've ever seen."*

> **—David Cooperrider,**
> Distinguished University Professor, Case Western Reserve University, Co-creator of Appreciative Inquiry

ACKNOWLEDGMENTS

WRITING THIS BOOK HAS BEEN a journey of healing and self-awareness. Christina and I became even closer by experiencing one another as co-authors. Our calling is to support individuals and couples seeking to enter into marriage. Every couple deserves to experience boundless love.

Our mission is to empower one million couples to flourish in their marriage by placing their faith in God as their foundation. We wrote this book because we know that our faith not only saved our marriage when we hit rock bottom, but transforms our lives every day in ways that we could never foresee.

For the last fourteen years, we served over 1,000 couples in our work with San Jose Catholic Engaged Encounter (SJCEE). These retreats were our boot camp, our classroom, and our refuge. We have no doubt that by serving God, we have grown immeasurably as individuals and as a couple. We want to thank this community, especially San Jose CEE, for being the pillar of what our marriage is today. You all are an inspiration and hold a special place in our hearts.

We are eternally thankful for Sheila and Luis Tuna for introducing us many years ago, Jav and Maricuz Islas for taking care of our Lucia during our most challenging time, Chuck and Rosella Blalock for believing in our dream, for Mark and Alise for their faith in our mission and being powerful role models in surrendering to God's plan.

Sunnyvale Christian School (SCS) has been our emotional rock and our spiritual family for over ten years. Both our girls started attending SCS in the two-year-old classroom (before there were actually two!). We grew in our faith and spiritual maturity because of the unconditional love in this community. Every teacher and staff member parented our children like their own and poured their love into our family. We are so thankful to have been lifted up by this special community. God worked through you and we are blessed in countless ways.

We are grateful for the inspiration of the Best Year Ever Blueprint (BYEB). We never knew that a book was possible, let alone inside of us until attending this powerful weekend. Thank you to Chandler Bolt of Self-Publishing School for speaking right to us that fateful weekend. Both Javier and I know that without this unique opportunity to envision our future together, "Boundless Love" would not be here today. Thank you for being so generous with your hearts in leading us to a better day.

We are additionally grateful to the Flourishing Leadership Institute (FLI), John Berghoff, and Nick Hemmert of The Center for Awesomeness for helping us to ask the right questions to dream and live change in our marriages. Knowing that the solutions are inside of us is more than half the battle and your practice of meaningful conversations transformed our family and our lives.

ACKNOWLEDGMENTS

And, finally, thank you, God, Jesus Christ. We would be nothing without you and we are so grateful to grow closer to you each day. May this book invite other couples to open their hearts to your devotion and care. We are forever thankful and blessed for your presence in our lives. Amen.

ABOUT THE AUTHORS

Javier Llerena

BORN IN MADRID, SPAIN, JAVIER Llerena has resided in the San Francisco Bay Area for the past thirty-five years. Founder of Re-Invent Coaching, Javier uses his over twenty years of international sales experience in high tech to provide strengths-based professional development to companies and individuals all over the world. He has been married to his soul mate, Christina, for over thirteen years and they have two daughters, Isabel and Lucia. Javier and Christina founded Boundless Love www.boundlesslove.us. A talented cook, accomplished marathon runner, and fourth generation Real Madrid Soccer Club fan, Javier is a hands-on father and devoted husband. Javier's advice is to surrender and trust God's path in your life. Cherish, protect, and be grateful for your family. God will do the rest.

Christina Llerena, MSW

ORIGINALLY FROM THE MIDWEST and alumni of University of Michigan, Christina transplanted to the Bay Area nineteen years ago from New York City where she earned a master's degree of social work from Columbia University. A community college professor and college admissions consultant, Christina co-leads Boundless Love, a couple's ministry with her husband, Javier Llerena. Their mission is to touch the lives of more than one million couples with Christ. Married for thirteen years and mama to Isabel and Lucia, Christina is a yogini, cinephile, and foodie. Christina's advice is to invite God to be your compass in life—let Him do the work and trust in His path. Be relentless in your self-care. You cannot give what you do not have—love yourself so you may love others exceptionally well.

CAN YOU HELP?

THANK YOU FOR READING our book!

We really appreciate all of your feedback, and we love hearing what you have to say.

We need your input to make the next version of this book and our future books better.

Please leave us an honest review on Amazon letting us know what you thought of the book.

Thank you so much!

Christina and Javier Llerena

Made in the USA
Columbia, SC
19 April 2021